P9-DEZ-652

DARE
TO
WIN

Berkley Books by Jack Canfield and Mark Victor Hansen

DARE TO WIN
THE ALADDIN FACTOR

Most Berkley Books are available at special quantity discounts for bulk purchases for sales promotions, premiums, fund-raising, or educational use. Special books or book excerpts can also be created to fit specific needs.

For details, write to Special Markets, The Berkley Publishing Group, 200 Madison Avenue, New York, New York 10016.

DARE
TO
WIN

JACK CANFIELD and
MARK VICTOR HANSEN

BERKLEY BOOKS, NEW YORK

DARE TO WIN

A Berkley Book / published by arrangement with
the authors

PRINTING HISTORY
Berkley mass market edition / August 1994
Berkley trade paperback edition / February 1996

All rights reserved.
Copyright © 1994 by Mark Victor Hansen and Jack Canfield.
Book design by Stanley S. Drate / Folio Graphics Co., Inc.
This book may not be reproduced in whole or in part,
by mimeograph or any other means, without permission.
For information address: The Berkley Publishing Group,
200 Madison Avenue, New York, New York 10016.

ISBN: 0-425-15076-3

BERKLEY®
Berkley Books are published by The Berkley Publishing Group,
200 Madison Avenue, New York, New York 10016.
BERKLEY and the "B" design
are trademarks belonging to Berkley Publishing Corporation.

PRINTED IN THE UNITED STATES OF AMERICA

10 9 8 7 6

Contents

Contents

Learn to Dare

In our dreams we all aspire to great things. Yet most of us simply aren't creating the results we want. We don't have enough money, romance, success or joy in our lives. Why not? What's holding us back?

The average person could probably list at least three good reasons to prove why he or she can't do whatever it is he or she really wants. But in the deepest recesses of our hearts, don't we really know that we could do it *all*—if only we dared?

Is it possible that the only main thing holding us back is *fear*? The answer is yes! It's fear that thwarts us, stalemates us, erodes our self-esteem and places imaginary roadblocks in our path. Fear keeps us from *taking action,* and if we don't act, we never get beyond where we are now.

But our fears *disappear* when we confront them. And once we take charge of ourselves, we can have, do and be anything and everything we've ever dreamed of.

We don't know what fears and self-doubts are currently keeping you stuck, but from our twenty years of experience in coaching hundreds of thousands of people, we do know that you can break through them and create everything you want. So let's start right now, today. Together, we can all *dare to win*.

Introduction

Amazing results! That's what we all want in our lives.

We might want more money. Or perhaps it's a more stimulating job we desire. Maybe it's true love, or a more gratifying
sexual relationship. We might secretly dream of being in the
movies, or of being president of a corporation, or even of en-
tering politics.

In our dreams we all aspire to greater things. Yet a great
many of us simply aren't getting the results we want. We don't
have enough money, romance, success or joy in our lives. We
don't feel fulfilled or satisfied. In some very deep and personal
way, we sense that we aren't living up to our full potential,
that we aren't winners.

Why?

Why aren't we all what we want to be? Why don't we have all that we want? Why aren't we prosperous and blessed with the world's abundance? What's holding us back?

If we ask the average person, I'm sure that he or she could give us plenty of "good" reasons for not succeeding:

I'm too ugly.
I'm too fat (skinny).
I'm too tall (too short).
I'm too old (too young).
I'm not smart enough.
I'm too weak.
I'm sick.
I don't have the education.
I'm from a minority group.
I'm bald.
I'm just a woman.
I'm just a wife.
I'm a single parent.
I'm a loser (two-time, three-time).

For most of us the reasons we don't have what we say we want, and can't get it, will be found in the litany above. Go through the list yourself and see if you can't immediately find at least three convenient reasons to *prove* that you can't do whatever it is you really want.

Are They Just Excuses?

Are those truly "good" reasons or are they just excuses? In the deepest recesses of our hearts, don't we really know that we could do it all—if only we dared? Don't we believe that we could have it all—if only we weren't afraid to go for it?

Are the excuses holding us back? Or is it that we just don't dare?

Think about it. Excuses are always there. But *daring*, that's inside, in our chest where that little hand grips our heart and tells us, "You're afraid!"

Afraid? Is it possible that the true enemy is . . . fear?

Fear? "I'm not afraid!"

In our culture we don't like admitting that we're afraid of anything other than direct physical violence. How could we be afraid?

Fear of Failure—or Success

We *all* have fears. For some of us it's fear of failure. If we try and don't succeed, then we fear we might embarrass ourselves. We fear that we might even embarrass other people.

For others, it could be fear of success. Succeeding might be even more *fearsome* than failing. If we succeeded in becoming president of that corporation, we'd have to speak before large groups, manage subordinates, produce annual reports, be responsible to stockholders. Could we handle it? Do we fear that we can't?

Danny DeVito, who's less than five feet tall, became a massively successful television star, movie star and director. He overcame his fears rather than let his fears overcome him. We all need to conquer our fears—one at a time.

If we became movie stars, could we handle the press, the critics, the work in front of the cameras? If we became prosperous, would we lose the friendship of our associates, the love of our family? Would we be breaking some unwritten code if we had more money than our parents, more than those we look up to?

Could hidden fears such as these be the real roadblocks? Could these—and not the excuses we mouth—be what's holding us back?

We submit that the answer is yes!

Fear of failure or fear of success, the simple truth is that most of us just don't dare to have, do or be what we really want. Nothing out there is holding us back. *We* are holding ourselves back.

Of course, almost no one would admit that to themselves. To protect our sensibilities, our subconscious cloaks our fears in perfectly reasonable-sounding excuses. We may indeed be bald, short, and wear thick glasses. Therefore, we tell ourselves that we'll never find the perfect mate, never be happily married.

You may be "just a woman," or "just a wife," or fat and tall, so your hidden mind reasons that you could never attain an executive position in a male-dominated corporation and rise to the top.

You're from the barrio, have little education and don't speak English well, so your unconscious figures you could never get a high-paying job.

You've gone bankrupt, lost all your money and possessions, so you tell yourself you can't start a major corporation, invest in real estate or tell others how to motivate their lives.

Right?

Wrong! You're listening to negative propaganda. You can't because you've convinced yourself you can't.

Getting Started

Fear limits us, thwarts us and stalemates us. The word "fear" may be seen as an acronym for False Evidence Appearing Real. It creates roadblocks and stumbling blocks and leads us into self-defeating behavior, which, in turn, produces guilt and anxiety, which can then lead to complete immobilization. Fear keeps us from trying, and if we don't try, we never get beyond where we are now—which in a convoluted way proves to us that we couldn't to begin with! After one of our seminars, a woman came up to complain that she couldn't go back to school because it would take five years to get a degree, and she'd be forty-three years old when she graduated. We couldn't help but ask her, "How old will you be in five years if you don't go back to school and don't get the degree?" A woman thirty-nine who just entered medical school will be forty-seven before she's on her own, but with a life expectancy of eighty-one, she'll have thirty-four fruitful years to make a huge contribution to society and herself.

The enemy is fear.

Fear erodes our self-esteem, corrupts our self-confidence and over time convinces us that we are losers. As long as we let our fear run us, we'll never *dare to win.*

The Way Out

Fear *can* be overcome and defeated—as long as we realize that the source of it is inside, not out there in the world. Franklin Delano Roosevelt addressed the subject eloquently in one of his fireside chats when he said, "The only thing we have to fear is fear itself." Napoleon Hill, author of the motivational classic *Think and Grow Rich,* who is attributed with authoring that line for Roosevelt, also wrote, "Confront your fears and you can make them disappear."

Once we realize that excuses don't count, we can begin to break through. Once we see that our subconscious fears—not external circumstance—are the real problem, we can take charge of ourselves and our lives. And once we take charge, we can be, do and have anything we want.

We all want to fully blossom and become the very best we can. We all want to have abundance and prosperity. We all want to make a difference. We all want to be robustly healthy and happy. We all want deep, purposeful and meaningful relationships. We all want love, joy, bliss and fulfillment. We all want the best of everything. We know that's what we want, and we know that's what you want. The miracle is that we can all have it! All we need to do is overcome our fears and dare to seek our goals.

Your Personal Breakthrough

Daring to win can happen all at once or it can be the result of a cumulative effort over time. We don't know what it will take to break through your particular fears. But we're positive that you can do it.

Our purpose in writing this book is to help you create an environment in your thoughts and beliefs that will allow you to make that breakthrough. We don't know if you'll begin to dare to win starting on page 17 or page 133, or two weeks after you finish the book.

But we know that you can! At this moment you don't have to believe you can do it, just believe that we believe you can do it. You can do almost anything if it doesn't violate the laws of God or the rights of other human beings.

DARE
TO
WIN

Problems Are
Opportunities in Disguise

*"Life is a grindstone, and whether it grinds you down
or polishes you up is for you and you alone to decide."*
—CAVETT ROBERT

"I've got a problem."

The young man had just come up to Dr. Norman Vincent Peale on Fifth Avenue in New York City, grabbed him by the lapels and said, "Dr. Peale, please help me. I can't handle my problems. They're just too much."

Dr. Peale said, "Look, I've got to give a talk. If you'll let go of my lapels, I'll show you a place where there are people with no problems."

The man said, "If you could do that, I'd give anything to go there."

Dr. Peale said, "You may not want to go there, once you see the place. It's just two blocks away." They walked up to the Forest Lawn cemetery and Dr. Peale said, "Look, there are

150,000 people in there. I happen to know that none of them
has a problem."

Problems Can Be Assets

That's one of Dr. Peale's favorite stories, and we've never forgotten his telling it to us, because it illustrates the true nature
of problems. Problems are a sign of life. If you have a big
problem, be thankful for it. It proves that you're alive and
functioning. (Some say, in fact, that the best way to judge a
person is by the size of the problems he or she has.)

The generally accepted viewpoint of most people, of course,
is that problems are bad. Most people feel that the ideal state
of things would be problem-free. Therefore, if we have problems, something must be wrong. As a result we end up devot-
ing a large part of our energies to bemoaning our fate. We end
up saying to ourselves, "Everything would be great, if only I
could just get rid of my problems!"

That's the pessimist's lament. The optimist, on the other
hand, sees problems as *opportunities*. If you've faced a severe
problem and broken through your fears in dealing with it,
you'll immediately know what we're talking about. But most
of us haven't done that, haven't broken through. As a result,
most of us just can't buy into the belief that problems can be
opportunities in disguise. Since we can't reach out and touch
you and talk to you personally about your own problems, we're
going to do the next best thing. We're going to show you several people who have had incredibly severe problems and the
amazing results that came from them.

Let's take four areas that people tend to worry about most,
where they tend to find their biggest problems:

Finances
Physical appearance

Multiple losses

Poor health

Financial Problems

We'll start with financial problems, since most of us can easily relate to them. Mark is our own best example here.

Back in 1974, when Mark was just twenty-six years old, he was building $2 million a year worth of geodesic domes in New York City. Geodesic domes, you'll recall, are triangles linked together to form large inhabitable units. They were invented by his mentor, Dr. R. Buckminster Fuller, and were the most famous of his two thousand major patents. At the time Mark was selling them as fast as he could make them.

But Mark had a problem. 1974 was the year of the first Arab oil embargo, and he was making the domes out of polyvinylchloride (PVC), a petrochemical (plastic) product.

It was definitely the wrong time to be doing that. When OPEC was formed, the price of oil products shot through the roof, and the Arabs said, "We can write checks so big that they'll make your banks bounce!"

It seemed as if one day he was on top of the world and the next he heard the judge saying, "Mark Victor Hansen, you are hereby declared bankrupt."

On the courthouse stairs before his trial date, a young attorney was soliciting his case. "Use my services," he told him. "For just three hundred dollars I'll file the bankruptcy for you." Mark said, "If I had three hundred dollars, I wouldn't be going bankrupt." To handle the case, Mark actually had to check a book out of the library called *How to Go Bankrupt by Yourself.*

That was Mark's all-time lowest hour. On a scale of 1 to 10, that was a minus 12. Mark got physically sick and felt like throwing up. Tears welled up in his eyes. His ears were temporarily blocked. He felt rejected and dejected, personally and professionally.

Mark climbed deep within a shell—permanently, he thought. He just had to lock out the world. Mark's escapist behavior included sleeping nearly around the clock. He went to bed at 6 P.M., lying to himself that he was tired, and got up again at 6 A.M. He was afraid everybody knew he had gone bankrupt, that he was a total failure. He was experiencing a form of escapist behavior.

Living with the Problem

Mark was bummed out. He tended to think of the humorous side of it. Just after going bankrupt, he parked at New York's Pan Am Building. The valet who retrieved his car looked at him standing there in the only suit the bankruptcy courts had left him, and said, "Man, I would have picked you for a Cadillac."

"Me, too," Mark said sadly.

He went from up to down in no time flat. Suddenly he was driving around New York in a four-hundred-dollar, pitted-window, permanently air-conditioned Volkswagen.

For a time he was unloading toilet paper off a railroad car in New York's freezing winter weather wearing a London Fog trench coat, a fine suit and patent leather shoes, earning $2.14 an hour. In the geodesic dome business, he was a salesman—an executive, a white-collar man. Now he asked himself, "Who am I?"

Hitting Bottom

During his lowest days, Mark would drive his junk heap into service stations and they would say, "Fill it up?" He'd say, "Twenty-five cents will do. Thank you." Mark was embarrassed and they were patient. Perhaps they could feel his predicament.

With his self-esteem completely trashed, he was at the bottom. But being at the bottom was his turning point—his time of greatest opportunity. He learned the principles we'll be sharing and teaching in *Dare to Win*. One of the keys is that no matter how bleak things are, never give up, there's always a way to solve every problem. After all, things couldn't get any worse for Mark—everything from there aimed up.

This is an important message to understand, and too often we miss it. We tend to look down on people who have gone bankrupt, to pity them. But in reality, the world at that point is totally open to them. They don't have to cling to any job they don't like, any business that doesn't fit them, any financial arrangement that traps them. The world is suddenly wide open to them. Everything is *potential*.

Starting Up

It was from being bankrupt that Mark would move up all over again. This time, however, he would learn the principles taught in this book and live by them from then on. "Mark," a friend told him later, "you burned your bridges behind you. You had to succeed!" Today Mark has a lovely wife, two beautiful daughters and an estate in Southern California. He owns three substantial businesses and is on the board of directors of half a dozen more. He travels 250,000 miles a year, having brought his messages of love, hope, courage, support and help to more than a million people.

We don't say all of this to brag about Mark, but to show you that even he could do it. Even he could turn a life around, from poverty to plentifulness. The very bottom, financially speaking, turned out to be nothing more than the very start of the rest of his life.

He had thought he had a problem, but it was really an opportunity. Going bankrupt was the best/worst experience he ever had. We say best because—given the insight of time and hindsight—bankruptcy got him out of building domes, which he shouldn't have been doing, and into professional speaking, writing and entrepreneuring, at which he is a master. Speaking, writing and entrepreneuring are Mark's natural livelihood, his "vocation with a purpose."

If you have what you think are financial problems, put them in perspective. They may be trying to tell you something. Ten years from today you may look back and see that they were in reality a tremendous life-changing opportunity. Allow us to *persuade* you that you can achieve wealth and financial freedom. It's absolutely available to you if you can be persuaded that it is and believe that you can achieve it.

But I'm Not Attractive Enough to Win

While financial difficulties may seem severe at the time we experience them, they are in truth some of the mildest problems/opportunities we are likely to encounter. After all, financial difficulties can almost always be solved with something rather simple and obvious: more money.

There are other kinds of problems that are far more intractable. Take, for example, our looks. Physical attractiveness—or its opposite, ugliness—is of almost universal concern. We think more people worry about their physical appearance than anything else about themselves. They consider it their biggest problem.

Haven't you ever been concerned about your physical attractiveness? Haven't you ever felt that maybe you didn't look quite as good as you should? Haven't some of the decisions in your life that have led you to where you are today been based on how you feel about your appearance? Haven't some of those decisions acted to hold you back, even just a little?

We suggest that our conception of our physical attractiveness to others can block us, and that's a real pity, because physical appearance has nothing to do with living an extraordinary life.

As proof we offer the following true story of Malcolm of Canada. Mark was giving a talk in Vancouver, B.C., a few years ago, and he happened to notice a man sitting in the front row who had the most mangled face he'd ever seen. He had stitches all the way across his face. One eyelid was stitched shut. Even his mouth was three-quarters stitched shut.

Mark remembers that he was talking about the importance of hugging, and at the break Malcolm came up and hugged Mark. With a raspy voice he said, "My name's Malcolm." Mark could tell from Malcolm's tone that he expected to be recognized, but if Mark had seen him before, he didn't know where or when.

He said, "I'm the guy who wrote you that letter."

He started telling Mark about it, and Mark remembered immediately. He had written that some ten years ago, he and his fiancée had been walking one weekend through the north woods of British Columbia minding their own business.

Somehow they had gotten between a mama bear and her baby cubs. The mama, just wanting to protect her cubs, had grabbed hold of his fiancée. Malcolm is just five feet two inches tall and the bear was enormous, but he felt courageous and managed to disentangle his fiancée, whereupon the mama bear grabbed him and proceeded to crush every major bone in Malcolm's body.

She finished by sinking her claws in his face and ripping straight across it, back toward the scalp.

It's amazing that Malcolm lived. He was in restorative surgery for the next eight years. By that time the doctors had done all the cosmetic surgery they could do. It hadn't helped much, and he saw himself as an ugly person. He didn't want to expose himself to society.

So he went in his wheelchair to the tenth-floor roof of his

rehabilitation center and was ready to push himself over the edge when his father appeared. His father had heard an intuitive voice telling him to go see his son.

Just in time, his father came running up to the top of the stairs and said, "Wait a second, son."

Malcolm turned around in the wheelchair. "What, Dad?"

His father said, "Malcolm, every human being has scar tissue deep inside him somewhere. Most of us wear it under a smile, some cosmetics and nice attire. You get to wear yours on the outside. But we're all the same."

Malcolm could no longer thrust himself off that building.

A short time later a friend of his brought him tapes of Mark's public appearances. He started listening and heard the story Mark tells of Paul Jeffers, who lost his hearing at age forty-two and has now become one of the most outstanding salesmen in the world. Mark heard it when Paul said, "Setbacks are given to ordinary people to make them extraordinary."

Malcolm said to himself, "That's me, I am extraordinary!"

He wrote down what he wanted to do. He dreamed about it and told everyone about it. Then he went out and got a job in insurance sales—a job where he has to expose his appearance to people every day. He puts his picture on his business cards, hands them to people and says, "I'm ugly on the outside, but I'm beautiful on the inside if you just get a chance to know me."

In 1978, Malcolm became the number one insurance agent in Vancouver.

Fate had dealt him a terrible hand to play. But he turned it into a golden opportunity.

You see, what Malcolm learned was that his looks weren't his problem. It wasn't his appearance that held him back. That was just an excuse. In life, one has excuses or results. It was his vision of himself that was the problem. If he saw himself as ugly, then he was ugly. But if he saw himself as beautiful, then he was beautiful. (Remember the old truth, "Beauty is always in the eye of the beholder, even if the beholder and person being viewed are one and the same.")

Once Malcolm "saw" what he *really* looked like, his scars became irrelevant. Once he broke through his fears by opening himself up to others, he was able to move forward with astounding results. So can you.

But I'm a Loser

"If you think you can or think you can't, you're right."
—HENRY FORD

A great many of us have a defeatist attitude. Usually the cause is that we've been put down so much for so long that we believe it's normal and natural for us to be put down. We can't win because we are the proverbial "born loser."

Once we define our problem as being a loser, how can we possibly win? We've eliminated the possibility of success. But having previously "lost" isn't the problem. It's how we view our losses. An optimist might say that we haven't yet succeeded.

Perhaps the most universally acclaimed example of this principle is Thomas Edison. Although Edison was thought of as an inventor, he didn't always enjoy the acclaim and respect in which he's held today. When Napoleon Hill interviewed Edison for the first time, he said, "Mr. Edison, what have you got to say about the fact that you've failed thousands of times in your attempts to create a light bulb?"

Edison replied, "I beg your pardon. I've never failed even once. I've had thousands of learning experiments that didn't work. I had to run through enough learning experiences to find a way that it *did* work." We all have had thousands of learning experiences; like learning to walk, we kept trying because we saw others succeed.

It's not that we are two-time, three-time, or forty-time losers. For most of us, it's just that we haven't had enough learning experiences to get it right yet.

For many of us, if just one experience doesn't turn out positively, we conclude that we're losers and give up trying. "I just can't do it," is the common conclusion.

Is it valid? To say that we can't succeed because we've failed once, twice or more in the past is nothing more than an expression of fear that we'll fail again. And as long as we have that fear, this roadblock of an excuse is going to be thrown up against us.

This is the time of no more put-downs, no self or other put-downs. Instead, encourage yourself and others.

As we've seen with Edison, it doesn't have to be that way. This is made even clearer through the true story of Bill Sands. Here is a guy who was given lemons and really did make lemonade.

Bill Sands had been a convict in San Quentin. When he got out of prison, he started writing, authored a book called *My Shadow Ran Fast*, about his experiences as a convict, and eventually became a public speaker. Mark had the privilege of listening to him one night when he was in college. Sands was in front an audience of about fifteen hundred students who, in their sophomoric innocence, thought they knew it all. Bill stood up there and said something like this: "My parents didn't like themselves. My father was a federal judge, my mother an alcoholic, and the only way I could get their attention was to do something like throwing a brick through a storefront window. Then I started robbing stores and got into more and more serious crimes and finally ended up in San Quentin.

"When I got there, they asked me to engage in perverted sexual activity. When I wouldn't, they broke my nose." At this point Bill pressed his nose flat to his face in front of those fifteen hundred students. "When they persisted and I resisted, they broke all the fingers in my hand." He bent all his fingers back ninety degrees.

Bill Sands had the attention of every one of those know-it-all students riveted on him. He continued with his story about feeling that he was the "losingest" person who had ever lived. Every one of us has shared that feeling or thought at some time in his or her life. Bill felt that losing was such a natural state of things for him that he couldn't conceive of anything different.

Then the warden, Clinton Duffy, took an interest in him. This warden read the histories of all the prisoners and saw something special in Bill. He gave him a copy of Napoleon Hill's book *Think and Grow Rich*, and Bill read the principles and read the ideas between the lines.

Bill decided that he was going to succeed—succeed by helping other prisoners. He wrote down his goals and talked about his goals, and even dreamed about his goals.

Even though he was in prison for life, Bill eventually was paroled, and he immediately started the Seven Step Foundation, which helped ex-convicts make it on the outside. He wrote his book about being a convict and talked about it on national tours such as the one Mark had attended at Southern Illinois University's Convocation Series. Almost instantly he became wealthy and successful.

By the time he was nearly finished speaking that night, he had made those students stand up, sit down, laugh, cry and decide to change their lives. (He was one of the reasons Mark eventually decided to go into public speaking.)

Finally, at the end of his talk, Bill said, "I want to introduce my wife, the most beautiful woman in my life." The curtain opened and she came out. Mark held his breath. With the arrogance of youth, he immediately decided that she was anything but beautiful. But the audience, women first, got up and gave her a standing ovation. As one, they seemed to say that if a great man like Bill Sands could see beauty in her, then she must indeed be beautiful.

Bill Sands, the losingest man who ever lived, by his own admission—and certainly by the condemnation of others—had become a personality so powerful that he could touch people to the very fiber of their being. He had seen through and cast aside that great excuse about losing that had kept him back. He had replaced a negative mental attitude with a positive mental attitude (PMA—it also stands for Pays More Always). He had taken a problem and found within it the seeds of an opportunity. His life's calling was not to be a convict. It was to be an author, a speaker, a businessman and a counselor. He had broken through. So can you!

I'm Too Sick

We hope that we've begun to touch a respondent chord in you with what we've written about the excuses we use to defeat ourselves. But we're sure you can relate to this last true story. It deals with sickness. We're not talking here about the hypochondriac who only believes that he or she is physically sick and is really just escaping from reality. That's also a problem of false images appearing as real, but not nearly as devastating as the one faced by somebody who truly is physically ill.

We believe we must maintain physical health if we're to keep our lives in balance and not constantly be distracted from the goals we set for ourselves. But sometimes health problems strike, and they can strike at any age. The real question then becomes: do we languish in our discomfort and our fear of staying sick, or getting worse? Do we give up? Or do we break through and continue to seek achievement and greatness for ourselves?

To illustrate our feelings on this subject, we'd like to briefly relate the story of Terry Fox. Terry's story was the subject of an HBO movie a few years ago. But somehow the film didn't quite get across the true impact of what he actually accomplished. We'd like to try.

Terry was a great Canadian athlete, lettering in several sports in college and looking forward to going into the pros. One day he started having trouble with his leg and went to a doctor. He found out that he had cancer; it was ravaging his leg. The doctor said, "I'm sorry, but we've got to amputate your leg. You're twenty-one, so you've got to sign off on your own leg." Terry bit the bullet and signed the form allowing his leg to be amputated.

Lying in the hospital bed convalescing over the next few days, Terry might have dwelt on his loss. He might have bemoaned the fact that his promising athletic career was finished even before it had gotten off the ground. But instead, he focused on a thought that someone, perhaps his high school coach, had told him, "You can do *anything*—if you do it with your whole heart."

Terry decided he wanted to run from one end of Canada to the other. His goal would be to raise a hundred thousand dollars and give it to youth cancer research so that other young people someday might not have to suffer the torment and travail that he had gone through. He wrote down his goal and thought about it constantly.

When he got out of the hospital, Terry was fitted for a false leg. He started hobbling around and started talking to everybody about helping to organize "Terry Fox's Marathon of Hope." He went to his mom and dad and told them what it was he wanted to do.

His father said, "Look, son, we saved our money and it's available to you—if you decide to go back to college. Once you graduate, then you can go and make a contribution." The next day Terry went to the Canadian Cancer Society and announced his intention of raising money through a marathon. They said they had to put it on the back burner because they were involved with a lot of other activities. They said his folks were right. "Skip it for now. Come back and see us sometime later. But thanks for thinking of it."

The very next day, he went to school and talked his college roommate into dropping out. The two of them flew out to Newfoundland. There Terry dropped his crutch into the Atlantic Ocean and started his cross-country run in Newfoundland.

Because he was an Anglo from British Columbia, Terry got no media attention at first. After 327 days, he finally broke into English-speaking Canada. By this time he was cruising farther than the Boston Marathon, more than thirty-one miles a day. The prosthesis wore heavy on the stump of his leg. Terry ran with a grimace across his face. The blood started trickling down and he started making front-page headlines!

Eventually he got to meet Prime Minister Trudeau. They shook hands and Trudeau asked Terry what he was really trying to do. Terry said his goal originally was to raise a hundred thousand dollars. "But with your assistance, Mr. Prime Minister, we can expand the goal to one million dollars." At first the prime minister didn't want to get involved.

That's when we started seeing Terry here in the United States. The TV show "Real People" went out and filmed him. You may have seen him carried by hockey players like Wayne Gretsky, across hockey rinks, while they raised buckets of money in the grandstands.

Terry kept on trucking. He got all the way to Thunder Bay in Ontario, where he began to develop deep respiratory problems. He went to check it out with an M.D., and the doctor said to him, "You've got to stop your run."

Terry told the doctor that he didn't know who he was talking to. He said, "In the beginning, my folks said I couldn't do it, and I chose to go ahead anyway. The Cancer Society told me no and I chose to go on. The provincial government has told me to stop because I'm clogging the highways. I chose to go ahead. The prime minister didn't really want to support me after I got a hundred thousand dollars, but finally he got behind it and we collected a million. When I leave your office, I plan to collect one dollar for every living Canadian—twenty-four point one million dollars."

The doctor replied that he sincerely wished that Terry could go through with it, but he explained that cancer was spreading densely through his chest. He told Terry, however, that he had inspired the country to drop its language barriers and provincial divisiveness. He had become the nation's hero.

He explained that there was a Canadian Air Force jet waiting at the runway to fly him home to Vancouver, where his parents would be waiting to take him to the hospital. Terry reluctantly agreed. We remember watching this on the evening news a few years later. They were rolling him into the emergency room, and a young journalist, hot for a story, practically jumped onto Terry's gurney and asked, "Terry, what are you going to do next?"

Terry was a pro to the end. He asked, courageously facing the camera, "Are you going to finish my run? Are you going to finish my run?"

He died a short time later. Ultimately, Canadians did raise $24.1 million for his fund.

Terry Fox's story is, to us, the most poignant case we can make for those who believe that they have a problem, and that the problem is keeping them from becoming a winner. If Terry showed us anything, he showed that there is opportunity for achievement even in the most desperate of situations.

Others might have seen Terry's illness as immobilizing. But he showed that just because we're sick doesn't mean we have to stop being human beings. Terry didn't use the excuse "I'm too weak and helpless. I've got too big a problem." Instead he broke through and dared to do something truly extraordinary.

> *"Every negative event contains within it the seed of an equal or greater benefit."*
> —W. CLEMENT STONE/NAPOLEON HILL

The World Is Filled with Opportunity

We doubt that your problems are nearly as severe as any of those we've described. But by taking extreme examples, we hope to demonstrate that even in the worst possible situations, those who dare can achieve amazing results.

In these examples, each person touched bottom. These people sank to the worst that could happen to them in terms of finance, physical attractiveness, multiple losses and ill health. But in each case the person didn't let that setback, that affliction, give him cause to roll over and succumb to his fears. Instead these people found, somewhere inside themselves, the courage to come back and *win*.

Indeed, in virtually every case, if there hadn't been a problem, that person might have continued on in the wrong job, with the wrong life, in a purely mundane manner. It's not that we're wishing problems on anyone. We're saying that every problem contains within it the seeds of an opportunity that could change your life. Problems can make us stretch mental, physical and spiritual muscles that we might never otherwise use, might not even know that we possess.

But I'm Not Like Them

Can you, personally, do the same thing yourself? If you have problems, as surely you must, can you see in them the same opportunities? Can you break through your fear, doubt, indecision?

Perhaps you're saying to yourself, "You guys have written about people who might be called 'super achievers.' But I'm not like that. I'm just an ordinary person without great courage. I don't have the drive or the spiritual resources to transcend my immediate problems and win great victories."

We respectfully submit that this is the ultimate excuse. To say that you can't do what others have done is the fear deep inside speaking for you. Why not ask yourself what it is you're really afraid of? Remember that the only way you're absolutely sure to fail is not to make the effort. So you really have nothing to lose but your fear of trying. And you've got everything to gain. Why not go for it?

Oh, What the Heck, Go for It Anyway!

A few years ago our friend Dr. Jack Wolfe taught us a very powerful technique. Whenever you are feeling afraid of going for it, and you are in the process of talking yourself out of doing what you know you need to do, close your eyes and repeat the following, out loud like a Gregorian or Buddhist chant: *"Oh, what the heck, go for it anyway!"* Repeat it again and again and again and take the right action to obtain the right result. Start by trembling if you must, but start!

2

Expand Your Imagination About What's Possible

"What things soever ye desire, when ye pray, believe that ye receive them, and ye shall have them."
—MARK 11.24

We're all born rich.

We're rich because we are born with incredible minds. We each have as standard operating equipment 18 billion brain cells. They ask only for direction.

To use our minds, we only have to tell them where we want to go, what we want to achieve. If we really know what we want, our minds can take us from where we are to where we want to be.

To see the mind's power in practice, ask yourself this question: "What did I really want five years ago?" If you were crystal-clear about what you wanted five years ago, then chances are you have it right now. How did you get it? Your mind brought you to it!

If you know exactly what you want, you can have it. So ask yourself, "What do I really want?" Do you know? If you're not crystal-clear about the answer, how can you get it?

The trouble is that most of us just aren't very clear about our desires. One of our favorite comic characters is *MAD*'s Alfred E. Newman, who says, "Most people don't know what they want, but they're pretty sure they haven't got it!"

This reminds us of the story of the farmer and the pilot. It was in the early 1920s, when barnstorming was the rage. They were having a fair in the Midwest and this pilot flew his bi-plane in. He had learned to fly in the Great War and was now scraping together a living by selling rides. His standing offer was one dollar per ride.

A farmer came up to him and said, "I want a ride, but I don't want to pay a dollar. Can we do business?"

The pilot thought a minute and offered this proposal. "I'll give you a free ride, if you don't say anything. If you don't scream or say one word or let out a peep, the ride's free. But if you make one sound, it's ten dollars. How's that?"

The farmer thought about it for a minute and said, "All right, I've got zipper lips. But my wife wants to go too. Can she get the same deal?"

"Sure," said the pilot. "But if she says even one word, it's ten dollars for her, too."

The farmer said, "We've both got zipper lips." So they took off. At twenty feet off the ground, the pilot turned the plane upside down and increased the speed. Then he went into a right-handed barrel roll, straightened and then a left-handed one. Then, double eights in the sky. By this time the plane was going at top speed. He pointed the nose up, and they climbed, climbed, climbed to several thousand feet— whereupon the plane stalled. It plummeted downward out of control until it was about twenty-five feet off the ground, when the pilot caught it and made a perfect three-point landing.

The pilot turned to the farmer and said, "That was amazing.

You never made a sound. I can't believe it. Wasn't there even one time when you wanted to say something?"

The farmer thought, then nodded his head. "Yep," he said. "When my wife fell out!"

Now there was a man who knew what he wanted. He was crystal-clear about it. Of course, we're not saying that we should all clam up in an emergency. We're only pointing out in a humorous way that what the mind wants, the mind gets.

How to Harness Your Mind's Power

We know that the human mind has two basic parts—the conscious and the subconscious. What we often fail to realize is that while the conscious makes all the decisions, the subconscious makes all the provisions. The conscious determines *what*, and the subconscious figures out *how*.

To put it another way, we all get out of life what we *expect* to get. If we expect a lot, we get a lot. If we don't put any *what* into our consciousness, the subconscious has a free ride and never has to worry about figuring out *how*.

Great thinking attracts great results. Mediocre thinking attracts mediocre results.

Each and every one of us has incredible resources of the mind. The school system teaches us how to use the brain— that is, it teaches us how to inventory and compute. But it barely touches the mind. The mind can think and go anywhere it wants to go. The mind can figure out where you are and take you where you want to be.

We decided that sooner or later we wanted to be able to speak to great audiences and to write best-selling books for people like you who care about the ideas we've got to share. We committed ourselves to this goal in our conscious minds, and our subconscious took care of the rest. You are reading one of the results.

As we said, you get whatever you expect to get. The only questions are "What do you want?" and "What do you expect from yourself?"

Actively Deciding

The exciting thing about using the mind is that we can short-circuit all the excuses thrown up by our fears. When we use our minds, creatively and constructively, it doesn't matter what we haven't done, what we haven't said, where we haven't been. The only thing that matters is how we engage the mind by telling the conscious what we want to do.

How high would you like to go?

Where would you like to be?

What would you like to have?

Whom would you like to meet?

We were afraid of the Russian space effort after they launched Sputnik. But John F. Kennedy made a conscious decision. He said that within ten years we would land a man on the moon. We did it in eight years and two months. The reason is, as Alfred Lord Whitehead said, "Great dreamer's dreams are never fulfilled, they are always transcended."

Everyone thought that Chrysler was going to go bankrupt, but Lee Iacocca said, "Chrysler will be the biggest and the best." Now he's America's hero. At Chrysler, he created vans that now account for 7 percent of all American auto sales. Iaccoca dreams big and inspires his dreams into realization.

We can have anything we want if only we dare direct our conscious mind to reach for it. The subconscious will figure out how to get there.

Crystallizing Your Goals

All you have to do is ask yourself, "What do I *really* want?"
Sometimes it helps to say it out loud. Pretty soon you'll hear
yourself replying, "I want this." As soon as you say that, you
will have engaged the conscious mind. You will have started
the ball rolling on the way to your desired result. You'll have
set a goal.

1. What do I want?
2. What do I really *believe* I have to do to get what I want?
3. When I do #2, I'll have #1!

Write It Down

Goals are like magnets. They pull us toward them. They are a
commitment to *do*. They set the subconscious mind to work.

The subconscious can be devious. If we still harbor hidden
fears and the subconscious realizes that its excuses aren't
working anymore, it has another trick it can use. It can make
us forget our goals. Today we decide that we're going to be a
corporate president. But tomorrow, in the day-to-day rush of
our lives, the goal seems to fade from our consciousness, and
the subconscious has a free ride again!

Therefore, as soon as we set a goal, we need to *write it
down*. Writing down a goal is a second act; it affirms that we
have taken action and makes that action permanent. It is a
concrete step. It makes it perfectly clear to the subconscious
that we're not fooling around, that we really intend to accomplish our goal.

It's important to note that we are only really thinking when
we are writing or computing our thoughts and distilling them
on paper.

When we write a goal down, we commit our whole mind to
following through. It's easy enough to overlook, pass by or

omit a goal that we once thought about, maybe whispered aloud and then quickly forgot. But it's a great deal harder when the goal is in black and white.

Write Too Many Goals

Many people will tell you to write down your goals, but we're different in that we tell you to write down *too many* goals. Don't just write down one or two goals. Write down dozens, at least 101 goals. We each keep a "Future Diary" in which we now have hundreds of pages of goals!

There are three good reasons to write down too many goals:

1. The first is that different goals have different gestation periods. A chicken egg takes twenty-one days to break into life, a human embryo takes nine months, and an elephant takes two years. Goals are like that. Some are accomplished quickly, some take many years.

   Back in 1974 when Mark started writing down his goals, he wrote that he wanted to have his own TV show. Now, that might have been considered an act of irrationality for a fellow who had just gone bankrupt. It takes at least ten thousand dollars to produce a half-hour show, let alone get it on the air. But the nice thing about writing down goals is that we can write down *anything* we want.

   Well, it wasn't until a good nine years later that Mark got a call from HBO for what turned out to be his first TV show. When the executive called to ask him, Mark said, "I've been expecting your call."

   The executive laughed and said, "How could you know I was going to call?"

   Mark replied, "Because I wrote it down nine years ago!"

   That goal took a long time to hatch. Others take only

a few days. We need a lot of goals so that some are always coming to fruition.

Another way of expressing this is to think of the universe as having its own perspective. What the universe sees, the universe eventually gets. Richard Attenborough conceived and wrote down the idea for the movie *Gandhi* fully twenty years before it was actually produced. He had set his goal and was ready for it immediately, but the universe wasn't. It took twenty years before people were ready to accept a movie about the great Indian leader. When the universe was finally ready, everything fell into place. Ben Kingsley was ready to act the role. (He was only a youngster when Attenborough conceived the movie!) Financing, marketing, distribution were abundantly ready. And so it happened.

Having many goals allows us time for the universe to catch up with our perspective.

2. The second reason to write down lots of goals is that when we reach a goal, it loses its power and importance for us. You enter mild to severe depression once you achieve a goal unless you've got another goal to go and get. If you wrote down that you wanted a new job and then you got one, the goal would become meaningless. It would be like a charm that had cast its spell and was worn out. So when we write down lots of goals, even though we accomplish some, there will be plenty more to keep our subconscious mind at work.

3. Another reason for not limiting ourselves to just a few goals is that the rule of the universe is abundance. Since you can have *everything* that you really want and are willing to work for, why settle for less? Mae West said it best when she said, "Too much of a good thing is wonderful!"

> **It's not that people want too much. It's that they want too little.**

Don't Compromise When You Write Your Goals

A lady Mark met in Seattle told him what goal setting had done for her. She'd just gone through a tragic divorce. She said she had heard Mark say that everyone should write down what they wanted, and not compromise about it.

After the divorce was final, she and two other ladies went to a cabin in the hills and spent the entire weekend writing down the qualities they wanted in an ideal man. She says she wrote out five pages more than the other women combined, so they copied hers!

She said that in addition to everything else, she wrote down, "And I want that man to have a Lear jet!"

The next day she went to a business meeting and there he was. She said it was just as though they had laser-beamed each other across the room. Within days they decided to get married. And the night before the marriage was to take place, her fiancé said, "Honey, there's something I haven't told you." She looked surprised and asked what it was. He said, "My daddy owns a bank and he's giving us the Lear jet to fly down to Palm Springs for the wedding." Emerson said to be careful what we dream about, because we're going to get it! Our mind moves forward once it has something to aim at, but it doesn't cost any more to set lofty, even inspiring goals. If you have incredible goals, you'll get incredible results. If you have no goals, your first goal is to set goals. Write outstanding goals and you'll build outstanding relationships and create outstanding results.

Here's a list of possible goals for someone who's just starting. It will give you an idea of what we're talking about:

1. Save a life.
2. Find a cure for cancer.
3. Win an Olympic gold medal.
4. Spend quality time with your friends and family.
5. Watch enriching TV programs.
6. Take vacations: Statue of Liberty; Yellowstone Park on a dogsled; horseback riding in Utah; white-water rafting in Colorado; tour all seven continents; Monte Carlo; safari.
7. Learn Spanish, a computer language and Chinese.
8. Go hot-air ballooning and fly a blimp.
9. Make yourself more attractive.
10. Develop a better sense of humor.
11. Develop a stronger memory.
12. Learn how to speed-read 3,000 words per minute.
13. Attain and maintain your ideal body weight.
14. Pay off all your bills and become debt-free.
15. Save $25,000.
16. Become financially free and independent.
17. Find your ideal spouse.
18. Have two children.

Don't Blab Your Goals

When you're a neophyte goal-setter, it's best not to tell the world your goals. If you do, others will shoot holes in them. In the beginning, it's preferable to share your dreams only with one or two others, as we said, who are like-minded and who will totally and unconditionally support you.

As you achieve more and more of your goals and begin to build up a track record of success and accomplishment, then you can tell the world about them, and others will emerge who can help you to realize your dreams.

Peter Ueberroth's stated goal of making the 1984 Olympics profitable through free enterprise attracted some to him, but produced a great deal of derision from many who pooh-poohed the idea. But when he was $150 million successful, he suddenly had credibility. Thus when he became the baseball commissioner, everyone believed he could and would accomplish whatever goals he set for himself in that job. When he stated publicly his goal of ending drugs in baseball, there were no disbelievers. Ueberroth says that "authority is 20 percent given and 80 percent taken."

Once you start achieving your goals and people see what you're doing, they'll start calling you outstanding, extraordinary, unusual and different. The point is not to invite discouragement early on by blabbing what you've set out to do. Do it and let your results shout for you.

When You Achieve Your Goals

When you achieve your goals, don't just cross them off. When we achieve our goals, we write "Victory!" Crossing off signifies that it's just a shopping list that's been easily handled. Writing "Victory!" signals the subconscious that it's a true achievement.

Additionally, our enthusiasm levels have peaks and valleys. When you hit a valley, you can look back over your peak experiences. You can look back at your victories as reinforcement toward new, greater and even more exciting peak experiences.

Goals are for a lifetime. They are our voluntary yet mandatory assignment.

Walt Disney had fifty-year goals. He died in 1966. After he died, Michael Eisner took over Disney and opened theme parks in Florida, Japan and France. Eisner expanded every part of Disney. Disney visualized it and Eisner has made it real as of this writing.

Have a Purpose

Goals are great, but by themselves they can be indiscriminate and undirected. Leaves fallen from a tree lie in a scattered heap on the ground. But leaves attached to a growing tree have the purpose of keeping that tree alive and healthy.

It's having an overriding purpose that makes the difference. A purpose is the underlying direction that gives meaning to our goals. We may have hundreds of goals—some of which we are continually achieving—but we may have only a single purpose that we spend our life working for.

> *"Life is not the sum of what we have been, but what we yearn to be."*
> —JOSE ORTEGA Y GASSET

Purposes are frequently spiritual in nature. The best example here is Christ. His spiritual purpose was simple, as stated in John 10.10: "I am come that you might have life, and that you might have it more abundantly."

As we've read these superstars biographies and autobiographies here are their self-exposed purposes: Disney's purpose: "To make people happy." Dr. R. Buckminster Fuller's purpose: "Humanity's comprehensive welfare on spaceship earth." Henry Ford's purpose: "To mass produce, mass distribute and have cars mass consumed." Andrew Carnegie: "To manufacture and market steel."

One purpose might be humanitarian. Mark was the commencement speaker recently at the graduation of Life Chiropractic College in Atlanta, Georgia. He met the oldest graduating doctor; she was seventy-two.

He hugged her, kissed her and said, "Doctor, before you came here to medical school, what did you do?"

"Until I was sixty-five," she answered, "I was a nun, and in my sisterhood, retirement at that age was mandatory."

"But why," he persisted, "did you decide at that age to spend the next seven years becoming a doctor?"

She replied humbly, "Because I wasn't done. My purpose is to serve." She is now seeing 150 patients a day.

We all need a purpose, and we need to put it down in writing so that we're crystal-clear about it. If you don't have a purpose, your first purpose is to get a purpose.

We have a purpose too. It's to empower, educate, entertain and enlighten as many people as possible without sacrificing our personal integrity or freedom.

Finding Your Purpose

To find your own purpose, our suggestion is that you go deep into yourself. Use meditation if you can. Go into the secret compartment of your mind and ask yourself, "If I knew my life purpose, what would it be?"

Keep asking yourself, and it will eventually unfold. Then you can easily write it down. To help you, here is a chart that shows the relationship of purpose to results:

PURPOSE = Why

GOAL = What

ACTION-STRATEGY = How

The "Why" is our purpose. It determines the "What," which is our goals. And our goals determine the "How," which are the actions and strategies we undertake to achieve the results we want.

Once you have your statement of purpose, your life will

become more meaningful. It could change your whole attitude. A crystal-clear statement of purpose that you act upon could mean the end of alcoholism, drug abuse, obesity, sleeping too much, a whole plethora of ills.

> *When you have a clear purpose, you won't have time for negativity.*

Abundance

If we don't have what we want, it's because we haven't asked for it. Look around you. The world is filled with abundance. Ask for almost anything and you will receive it.

This chapter is, in reality, a time machine. It can release you from the constraints of wanting, but not having. All you need to do is ask the crystal-clear question and wait for your mind to make it happen.

3

Focus Your Energy

Success is creating a state of mind that allows you to obtain whatever it is you really want.

Dr. Victor Frankel (author of *Man's Search for Meaning*) was one of the few survivors of Auschwitz. He was a German Jewish psychiatrist who somehow managed to live where tens of thousands of others died. With little food or clothing and no medical attention, he was forced to stand by while his fellow prisoners were cremated.

Upon being released at war's end, he was asked how he

had managed to survive. What powers did he have that others lacked? How had he managed to stay alive?

He is said to have replied, "I always knew that my attitude was my own choice. I could choose to despair or to be hopeful. But to be hopeful I needed to focus on something I wanted.

"I focused on my wife's hands. I wanted to hold them one more time. I wanted to look into her eyes one more time. I wanted to think that we could embrace again and be heart to heart one more time. That kept me alive second by second by second."

Dr. Frankel did not have more energy available to him than the others at Auschwitz. He said that frequently his entire food ration was one pea in a bowl of soup. But rather than uselessly expend that energy in despairing at what was happening to him and those around him, he focused it on a single goal. He gave himself a reason to survive, and by concentrating on that reason, he was indeed able to survive.

He created an attitude of hope for himself. Once his attitude was positive, his mood took care of the rest. It automatically said, "Today, in order to survive, you must do this and this and that." As long as he stayed focused, he was a survivor.

Focusing

Focusing our energies in a single direction can work for us just as it worked for Dr. Frankel. If we want something enough, and if we keep our mind focused on getting it, we will eventually achieve it. Mark reflects:

This was brought home to me at a relatively early age by my father. My dad came to the United States from Denmark in 1921. He was seventeen years old, had an eighth-grade education and was trained as a culinary artist to decorate gigantic cakes and other specially ordered baked goods.

My father was immediately impressed by the United States as a land of opportunity. Unlike other countries, here you could want something, work for it and get it. He worked hard and while we were never rich, we also were never poor. Dad always said:

> *The free enterprise system means that the more enterprising you are, the freer you are.*

When I was nine years old, just old enough to ride a bike well, I got a job delivering newspapers, carrying them in a sack from house to house. From my newspaper route I earned enough money to buy a bicycle magazine, and I devoured it month by month. Long before European bicycle racing gained popularity here, I knew all about the bike styles, the lowered handlebars and racing bikes with thin tires and narrowed seats. I felt that I could be a great cyclist. I was missing only one thing—a racing bike.

I determined that my foremost goal in life was to get a racing bicycle. I wanted this bike with my whole heart, mind, body and spirit. I had an ideal bike in mind. It was made in England and to this day I can remember the company's slogan, "Ride a wheel on Sheffield Steel!"

From the magazine I cut out a picture of the bike, and I kept it next to my bed. Nightly, I went to sleep dreaming about how I would be pedaling four hundred miles a week to get into great shape for long-distance bicycle races with the Windy City Wheelers between Chicago and Milwaukee. I could see that bike. I could feel it. I believed it.

> *Focused mind power is one of the strongest forces in the universe.*

But when I went to my father and asked for the bike, my father didn't understand my desire. After some discussion, my dad said, "You can have it when you're twenty-one years old."

"Twenty-one! I'd be an old man by then!" I told him. "You don't understand, I don't want a bike when I'm twenty-one, I want it now!" (Children don't believe in deferred gratification!)

I kept badgering my father and finally got him to concede to me getting a bike by the age of sixteen. This, I saw, was as far as he was going to bend. So I brought up an old favorite of my father's, the free-enterprise system. I said, "Can I have the bike now if I earn the money to buy it myself?" I'm sure my dad never dreamed that a nine-year-old could earn the huge amount of $175—today roughly equivalent to $1,075—so he had little to lose and he agreed.

I wanted that racing bike so badly that in my mind I already owned it. It's important to totally believe you can achieve your heart's desire. I even visualized cleaning and waxing it weekly. I could almost touch it. I had engaged my mind power. Inside every human mind/brain complex are abilities that go beyond the normal. These abilities are tapped when we have a white-hot desire. They figure out how to get whatever we really want to get. My mind power made it possible for me to see an advertisement in *Boy's Life* magazine promoting the sale of Christmas cards on consignment. Instantly my mind made me believe that I could nb sell the cards.

I went to my mother, who was a phenomenally good saleswoman. She had charisma, beauty, a radiant smile, a sincere interest in people, and she was a master storyteller. I asked her if I could sell. She said, "Not only can you sell, but I'll teach you how! It's important to have a smiling face, see a lot of people and ask everyone to buy your greeting cards. But it's most important to use the 'alternate choice' close. Ask your potential buyers, " 'Would you prefer *one* or *two* boxes of Christmas cards?' "

So I began. I approached my neighbors in the early winter of 1957, with deep snow on the ground, wearing a blue-hooded parka, a cold red face and big furry mittens. I went door-to-door every day, and when a mom answered the door, I would wipe my nose on a mitten and ask her if she'd like to buy some cards. How could she refuse that cute little kid with a runny nose? Generally she'd say, "Young man, come in here. We can't let you stand out in the cold."

Once I got inside, I knew the sale was made. I would explain that I was earning money for my own bicycle. Then I'd ask, "Mrs. Shaw, would you prefer *one* box or *two*?"

I was a great salesman. But it's important to understand exactly what I was doing. I didn't want to sell 376 boxes of Christmas cards. I had no desire to be the number-one greeting card salesman for American Greeting Cards in the nine-year-old division. I didn't enjoy going door-to-door in the cold. I wasn't interested in any of those things. I was getting my bike, which I did.

Focusing Produces Results

Mark continues: I learned a lot from this experience. I learned the importance of working hard to get what you want. And I learned how to handle money. (And after my father took half of what I earned and put it into savings for college, I learned the importance of savings.) But most important of all, I learned that if I really wanted something and focused my energy on it, I could tap into my mind power. My mind power would show me the way, instruct me in what to do, so that I could have exactly what I wanted. Once you know what you want, the resources of time, money and people show up.

This was undoubtedly the most important lesson of all.

Visualization

We hope we've convinced you that focusing our energy really does work. The technique we use is actually called *visualization*. First we visualize what we want, then we achieve it.

When Arnold Palmer sinks a golf ball, he has said he first visualizes it going into the hole.

William Zeckendorf, the real-estate multimillionaire, told a journalist he visualized a magnificent building for the United Nations in the heart of New York City. A few short years later, he built it. We recommend you put it on your goal list to visit for a day.

Aristotle Onassis always said he was a persistent dreamer/schemer. He said he "saw" his first ship in his mind long before he acquired it. He "saw" himself controlling a fleet of oil tankers before he achieved their ownership.

Jack La Lanne, the health and fitness king, says he visualized himself as going from a lightweight, unwell youth to a robustly healthy man who would gain fame and fortune by promoting health to others. He's a walking, talking advertisement for the gospel of good health, and has been on TV promoting it for more than forty years. He's even successfully promoting juicers on a TV infomercial.

Your belief determines your action, and your action determines your results. Better feedback from your results generally improves your attitude and future new results. But first you have to believe.

The list of those who have succeeded by first visualizing their success is almost endless. And it doesn't apply just to the rich and famous—although if you keep using it as a principle, you'll probably end up that way yourself!

Motivational authority Zig Ziglar tells the story of a fellow who came to a seminar he was teaching. The guy said aloud that he thought it was all bunk. He was an enormously fat man, more than 450 pounds. He probably would have left, except that it was difficult for him to stand up and slip out in front of all the people there.

The fellow went home and started seeing himself thin. He started seeing himself weighing 250 pounds, and he saw himself physically fit. He believed he would be wearing a size 46 suit. And over the next six months he lost a lot of weight.

He knew he was a success when one day he was in a shopping center and a little girl said, "Look, Mommy, a fat man!"

He turned around automatically and to his heartfelt gratification saw that the little girl wasn't pointing at him, but at someone else!

Visualize Completely

It's important, when we are first introduced to visualization, that we understand that we must visualize *completely*.

Carl Lewis told reporters he visualized that he would match Jesse Owens's historic record at the Olympics. He felt that he would then gain fame and fortune through endorsements. Well, he got what he visualized by equaling Owens's record. But he got very few endorsement offers after the Olympics, and many have already forgotten his name. In our opinion, the problem was that he visualized himself only as matching Jesse Owens's record; he should have visualized himself as *breaking* it. Then he'd be known as the all-time Olympic record holder, and the recognition would have been instantaneous and massive.

Perhaps the best example of complete visualization is Walt Disney. Disney envisioned the movies he created before they were filmed. In fact, he was one of the developers of "storyboarding," the art of creating a complete story line on art boards before even beginning a movie.

Walt "saw" before he acted. He "saw" Disneyland in Anaheim complete before it was ever built or the ground for it purchased. He "saw" Epcot Center in Florida and Disneyland in Japan, and Disneyland in Paris, yet they weren't built until years after he died.

Walt visualized completely. He knew that it doesn't cost any more to dream big than it costs to dream small. He understood, more clearly than anyone we've ever heard of, the power of visualization.

The two of us work together on many projects simultaneously and we storyboard what we want, on a gigantic white wall. We put yellow Post-its on the wall declaring our "to-do's." We later prioritize them and mark off our victories whenever we get together.

You Create Your Own World

Disney is reputed to have required his staff to meet every morning at 7:30 at their Burbank studios and follow this ritual: They would point to their temples and say, "My imagination creates my reality."

How right he was. The world we live in is the combined images of all of our human minds. We have made the world into what it *seems* to be for us. We fly, have cars and houses, sleep in beds, have air-conditioning, spend money, go to work in the morning, not because all this is part of the natural order of the universe, but because we *invented* it. First we visualized it and then we collectively caused it to exist. If we stop believing that all these things exist, then they'll stop existing for us.

There is no time and no space. There is only our minds and what they create. (That's why, for example, the world as seen by the Native Americans, with its animal powers, was so different from our own.) This is best seen and understood in a brilliant film called *The Gods Must Be Crazy*. We encourage you to get it at your video store or public library. It shows a pygmy tribe living in peace and harmony in the Kalahari Desert, when a pilot throws a Coke bottle in their midst and totally disturbs their serenity and tranquility. It's a mind-expanding, humorous story.

No one saw this more clearly than Socrates, who could often be found sitting outside the city of Athens greeting strangers. One day a stranger came up to him and said, "I would like to live in your city. What kind of people does it have?"

Socrates replied, "What kind of people are in the city you've come from?"

To which the man replied, "Oh, they're not very nice. They lie, cheat and steal. That's why I'm moving out."

Socrates, in his wisdom, replied, "It's the same way here. If I were you, I'd keep looking."

A short time later another man came up and asked about the people in Athens. Socrates again asked the man about his own city. The second man replied, "They're wonderful. They always help each other. They're truthful and industrious. I just thought I'd like to see other parts of the world."

Socrates, in his wisdom, replied this time, "It's the same way here. Why don't you go into the city? You'll find it just as you imagine it should be."

When we move, we bring our attitudes, ideas and images with us wherever we go. Why not work to improve them now and always, in all ways?

> *It has been said that the great mandate of our world is not to set things right, but to see things right.*

Seven Steps to Visualization

Visualization is the process of seeing within your mind. It is one of the most powerful principles available for creating your future. It works to convert sickness into health, fat people into thin people, losers into winners. It even works to help governments turn the economy around.

This latter use was made clear when Abe Beame was mayor of New York. He seemed to lack both the power of visualization and vision. The day Mark went bankrupt, nineteen thousand people were laid off across the city, and Mayor Beame announced that New York City itself was going bankrupt. That kind of thinking and verbalization repels businesses.

It almost did. Then the city got a new mayor, Ed Koch. Mayor Koch said business was great. He "saw" that business was great. Thinking positively—in terms of possibilities instead of doom and gloom—he began *acting* positively, and before long business started coming back to New York—and it *was* great again. Positive thinking, believing, speaking and achieving attracts business—personally, corporately and governmentally.

The power of visualization is limited only by your resourcefulness.

We all visualize naturally to some extent. Most people, asked to close their eyes and see their car, their homes or their refrigerators, can do so easily and effortlessly. Even blind people tell us they can see/feel their life experiences. The problem is that most people project only negative visualization:

"I hope I don't get the cold she has."
"What if I have an accident?"
"God, what if I can't pay my mortgage?"
"My parents will kill me if they find out I'm pregnant!"
"He won't call."

"I'll be late and get fired!"
"Everything I eat turns into fat!"
"I'm not good enough."
"There are no parking spaces left."

These folks expect bad results. Why are they surprised when they arrive?

We need to practice positive visualization if we want to produce positive results:

"I'm healthy and I'm going to stay that way!"
"My bills always get paid!"
"He'll be calling soon."
"I watch what I eat carefully, and it keeps me trim."
"I'm a terrific person!"
"I'm happy."
"I'm successful."
"I'm loving, loved and beloved."

With such positive visualizations, can positive results be far behind?

One Thought at a Time

Since we won't always be visualizing some specific goal, it's important that we create a bountiful master visualization that allows us to grow, develop and flourish in every area of our life—health, family, finance, social life, recreation, spiritual and mental acuity. It should become a habit. We should practice thinking, feeling and seeing positively.

Many of us already visualize, but we do it in the form of a bad mental habit. Like worrying, for example. When we're not focused on some specific task or train of thought, we tend to lapse into a state of nonproductive and negative worry.

Your mind can only hold one dominant thought at a time. Think positively, creatively, imaginatively and constructively.

To replace a bad habit like worry, we need to transplant in its place a good habit like visualizing ourselves as calm, cool, poised, centered and collected, in every situation. Since we own our imagination, we can discipline it positively and correctly if we decide to do it.

The Visualization Process

This process is not only painless but joyful. You can use it to open up your life to widening horizons, to purposes and possibilities that will enable you to serve yourself and your fellow man in increasingly wondrous ways.

STEP 1

The Inhalation Step:
Relaxed Awakeness

Put yourself in a comfortable position, perhaps sitting in your favorite chair. Have music gently playing in the background at sixty beats per minute, baroque music like Pachelbel's Canon in D or music like Dr. Stephen Halpern's *Spectrum Suite*. Great music deepens and enriches the experience. The best position, if you can master it, is the Indian lotus position, cross-legged on the floor with the palms of your hands upward, your ankles on your thighs. This posture, once mastered and made comfortable, affords the body the best circulation and most concentrated use of the mind. If it's too difficult for you, you may sit in a chair or lie on your back.

Should you choose to recline in bed, push back sleep until you're finished creatively visualizing. Then it's okay to fall immediately into a deep sleep.

When you're positioned comfortably, begin inhalation. This is deep breathing that relaxes you totally and absolutely. Inhale through your nose (take in this breath s-l-o-w-l-y while concentrating on the experience of inhaling).

While you're inhaling, notice the life-force energy of the air you're breathing. It has the potential to empower you once you recognize it. Fill your lungs, and hold it for thirty seconds, silently affirming to yourself, "I am relaxed." Then exhale through your mouth. Then take another breath and with each inhalation take the breath deeper into your body. Most people breathe in a very shallow way. Really *fill* your lungs.

While you're holding your breath this time, silently state the affirmation, "I love, am loving and beloved."

You should feel the intoxication of your spirit with this ingestion of oxygen and the verbalization of love.

On the third inhalation, feel your breath fill every atom of your being. Suck the air all the way into your toes, hold it for 30 seconds—affirming silently, "I am totally self-confident"—then *slowly* let it out.

As you continue practicing this exercise on a daily basis, your body, mind and spirit will begin to come alive in new and wonderful ways. Since most of us are living far below our potential because no one has awakened us to it, this technique allows us to *suddenly* sense what we *might* be, and thus it becomes positively addictive, once fully experienced.

Now resume normal breathing and proceed to Step 2.

STEP 2

Open Your Inner Eye to the Stage of Your Imagination

The inner eye is the eye of vision and imagination. All of life is created in the workshop of this eye.

An opened inner eye is essential to our growth as a fully

functioning, no-limit, self-actualizing person. With our inner eye open, we can "see," or visualize, all that we can become.

To begin, picture yourself on the stage of a theater (if you have trouble "seeing" yourself, you may need a favorable photograph of yourself that you can glance at just before you close your outer eyes). Your pictured self is center stage while you (in the audience) sit watching. Lights up, curtain up—action!

Now make your stage self begin acting out whatever it is you want. Perhaps you'd like to have a new car. Allow your inner eyes to produce the car on stage. Your stage self drinks in the deep color, runs his/her hand over the polished surface. You see your stage self get into the new car and smell that "new car" odor. You turn on the engine and the stereo, feel the steering wheel, and away you go as you press the accelerator of your new car.

As you gain expertise with this stage technique, you can graduate to picturing yourself in the movies or on video! Now the limitations of a stage setting disappear. You can use your imagination and be out driving that car across snowy mountains and through green fields. You may even advance to the point where you have split screen or 3-D images!

Another variation is to imagine walking down to the stage or into the movie and becoming one with the self you were previously observing. Psychologists call this "associated" visualizing, which is more powerful than the "disassociated" observing. Once again make sure you include sounds, feelings, sensations and smells. Include all of your five senses as much as possible.

STEP 3

Use Your Past Experiences

Once we've advanced to the point where we can visualize the future we desire, we can move on to the next stage, which allows us to call on past experiences to help us actualize that future.

Our minds are like a videotape library. They contain a complete record of all our experiences. This fact kept Captain Gerald Coffee alive in a POW concentration camp in Vietnam for seven years.

Captain Coffee began by visualizing repeatedly what it would be like when he was free again. He then recalled old "videotaped" images from his past, when he was free. Finally he superimposed one on the other. The resulting visualization, which he did day and night, was so total that he was able to stay alive and sane until he was finally freed in reality.

Captain Coffee visualized that he had faith in America, faith in his fellow servicemen, faith in God and faith in himself. He visualized that he would teach about that when he was released. He is a magnificent speaker and helps people understand why our military peacekeepers are important. We hope you make a goal to hear Captain Coffee speak. Call him at (808) 488-1776 for his speaking schedule.

We can use our minds to play back experiences and impressions that we've recorded almost since we were born. We can then use these recordings to embellish, solidify and give power to the goal we're visualizing.

This is easy to do. While focusing on your particular goal, let into your mind seemingly extraneous but nevertheless relevant thoughts. The mind acts like a gigantic filter. It goes back through our past experiences and brings to the surface memories that might be useful in the future.

STEP 4

Change the Past

The good news is that if you don't like the video being played across your mind, you can change it!

> *It's never too late to have a happy childhood, or a*
> *happy life experience.*

You can reproduce, rewrite, review and rescript what happened in the past and make it the way you want it to be. For example, not long ago Mark and his wife took up downhill skiing. She loved downhill, but hated cross-country. ("It's too much like work!") Mark, on the other hand, was just the opposite. He loved cross-country and feared downhill. ("I'm afraid I'll crash into a tree!" Mark said.)

Each of these reactions could have been predicted if Mark and his wife had been able to run the old tapes that were locked into their minds. Because buried deep within our subconscious are the seed thoughts that grow and rule our present.

Mark was determined to try downhill, even though he feared it. Then, when he got on the ski lift, disaster hit. Arriving at the top of the mountain he "inadvertently" plunged his right ski into the hardened snow and somersaulted right on top of Bogus Basin in Idaho.

He was humiliated, hurt and chagrined as the lift operator stopped and suspended all the skiers on the chair-lift in midair, allowing him time to struggle to his feet. He finally stood up, but his skiing abilities stayed down.

Mark's mind was visualizing everything going wrong by this time, but he knew how to snowplow, so he did just that—fearfully, hesitantly and sweatily—all the way down the mountain, even though he was being watched and helped by an experienced teacher who constantly kept reassuring him that he really could do it.

His fear was greater than his faith on that trip. He puzzled over the why of it. He had cross-country skied in Estes Park,

Colorado; Lake Tahoe, California; Mount Hood, Oregon; Fair-banks, Alaska; and many other places, and had done it very well. So why could he not even begin to get started on downhill skiing?

Mark used the visualization techniques described here to focus on downhill skiing. While doing so, he allowed other videos to surface in his memory. To his amazement, what popped into his mind was a movie that he didn't even know he owned and that he had input years earlier. It showed a person he was very close to who had crashed into a tree and had been put into a cast from head to toe.

That experience in his subconscious was keeping his fear level high and preventing him from becoming any sort of downhill skier. So in the theater of his mind, he pulled out his brain-cell video titled "Downhill Skiing." He metaphorically opened the video container, pulled out the tip of the old tape, lit a match to it and burned it up and out of his experience.

He then inserted a new blank tape. Using his imagination, he rewrote "Downhill Skiing." He "saw" himself as an expert skiing down the slopes. Using the techniques that will follow, he made it vivid. Then he programmed in the exhilarating feeling he experiences when he cross-country skis. He saw himself—wonderfully poised, tremendously excited and vi-brantly alive—going downhill . . . without fear!

Then he tried downhill skiing once again, and this time it was a success!

Eighteen Holes in His Mind

Major James Nesmeth, whom Bert Decker writes about, had a dream of improving his golf game—and he developed a unique method of achieving his goal. Until he devised this method, he was just your average weekend golfer, shooting in the mid to low nineties. Then, for seven years, he completely quit the game. Never touched a club. Never set foot on a fairway.

Ironically, it was during this seven-year break from the game that Major Nesmeth came up with his amazingly effective technique for improving his game—a technique we can all learn from. In fact, the first time he set foot on a golf course after his hiatus from the game, he shot an astonishing 74! He had cut twenty strokes off his usual average without having swung a golf club in seven years! Unbelievable. Not only that, but also his physical condition had actually deteriorated during those seven years.

What was Major Nesmeth's secret? *Visualization.*

You see, Major Nesmeth had spent those seven years as a prisoner of war in North Vietnam. During those seven years, he was imprisoned in a cage that was approximately four-and-a-half feet tall and five feet long.

During almost the entire time he was imprisoned, he saw no one, talked to no one and experienced no physical activity. During the first few months he did virtually nothing but hope and pray for his release. Then he realized he had to find some way to occupy his mind or he would lose his sanity—and probably lose his life. That's when he learned to visualize.

In his mind, he selected his favorite golf course and started playing golf. Every day, he played a full eighteen holes at the imaginary country club of his dreams. He experienced everything to the last detail. He saw himself dressed in his golfing clothes. He smelled the fragrance of the trees and the freshly trimmed grass. He experienced different weather conditions—windy spring days, overcast winter days, sunny summer mornings. In his imagination, every detail of the tee, the individual blades of grass, the trees, the singing birds, the scampering squirrels, the lay of the course became totally real.

He felt the grip of the club in his hands. He instructed himself as he practiced smoothing out his downswing and the follow-through on his shot. Then he watched the ball arc down the exact center of the fairway, bounce a couple of times and roll to the exact spot he had selected—all in his mind.

In the real world, he was in no hurry. He had no place to go. So in his mind he took every step on his way to the ball, just as if he were physically on the course. It took him just as long in imaginary time to play eighteen holes as it would have taken in reality. Not a detail was omitted. Not once did he ever miss a shot, never a hook or a slice, never a missed putt.

Seven days a week. Four hours a day. Eighteen holes. Seven years. Twenty strokes off. Shot a 74.

Can It Really Be That Easy?

Those who are unfamiliar with the technique we've just described may find it incredible. If you feel that way yourself, we offer another example, one that has received some spectacular publicity in recent years.

What we're speaking of is "rebirthing." Rebirthing is a psychological regression technique, created by Leonard Orr and Sondra Ray, that takes us back to the time we were born. If there was pain, anguish, trauma, hatred or hurt, the rebirther can help us overcome it.

Mark happened to be in Hawaii on a speaking tour, and one of his fellow speakers asked permission to bring in a rebirther. Mark had heard of fantastic results from rebirthing, but he was skeptical and thought it was perhaps nothing more than psychological mumbo jumbo. But he agreed to go through it along with sixty others.

They went through deep breathing as a group. Then, with their express permission, they individually entered into a deep hypnotic trance watched carefully by the rebirther. Within seconds Mark found himself in a fetal position. To his amazement he clearly experienced himself watching on two screens of his imagination simultaneously, something that he'd never previously done.

He was both the man he is now and the infant he was at birth, still inside his mother, something that Einstein called "all at oneness." Mark's birth had been pleasant. His mother had been told by the doctors that she couldn't get pregnant again after the birth of his older brother. But she did, with Mark and his little brother, and she wanted them so much that she called them "miracle children."

The rebirthers said that if one's birth was a "piece of cake"—as Mark's was—they should beam their memories forward to a time of possible/probable complication, and then work on it.

Mark's mind light-beamed forward to age three on a Sunday afternoon. It was his father's only day off from the bakery he owned and operated with a vigilant Puritan work ethic. He was lying on their sofa holding him and hugging him.

As a baker he had contracted painful, knuckle-expanding and motion-restricting arthritis. In pre-verbal empathy for his dad, Mark feelingly stated, "Daddy, you don't have to have that arthritis. I'll take it from you." In his youthful naivete, he locked into an erroneous belief that would have ultimately created arthritis in his own body. As he looked at that in his rebirthing state, he started sweating profusely.

Mark remembers one of the rebirthers comforting him with a cool towel and repeatedly saying, "Release it and let it go, permanently. It's over and done with." He did . . . and it was! He banished from the kingdom of his awareness that sick thought and along with it the possible beginning of his future arthritis.

Note: rebirthing and psychological regression techniques should be administered only by practitioners who you know are trustworthy, have integrity and no vested interest. If you are going to use this sophisticated visualization technique, get a master to lead you over, under, around or through your blockages.

Rebirthing is an extreme example of rewriting the script. To a much lesser degree, we can do it ourselves by the method we've suggested. Just find the negative video and give it a new script. It worked for Mark for downhill skiing, to name only one instance. It can work for your goals as well.[1]

STEP 5

Use All Your Senses

When you make or remake a videotape of the imagination, employ all five of your senses—taste, touch, smell, vision and hearing. Each modality you use will heighten the impact of the process.

Make sure you use all of your senses individually. For vision, make your imagined screen as big as the best movie theater you've ever pictured. Make it alive with the vibrant technology of this scientific age.

Add the equivalent of Dolby or Lucas sound so that you can hear everything perfectly.

---

[1]You can re-create your childhood using sophisticated NLP (Neurolin guistic Programming) techniques. Jack Canfield and Tim Piering have created a powerful rescripting process on audio cassette. You simply close your eyes and follow the process. The tape is called *Restructure Your Childhood*. Call 1–800–2ESTEEM or send $15.00 to The Canfield Group, 6035 Bristol Parkway, Culver City, CA 90230.

Allow aromas to suffuse your olfactory senses.

Touch it. Feel the texture, the grain, the warmth (or cold-ness) of it.

If it's edible, taste it. Put it to your tongue and imagine its taste.

Now combine the senses in one glorious sensual experience of what you're imagining. If it's freshly made organic carrot juice, smell the aroma and enjoy the taste. Look at the dark orange color and feel it go down your throat, nourishing you at a cellular level.

For those who are just starting, sometimes it is easier to first determine which of your inner senses is the most sensitive, and then start with that. For example, if touch is the easiest for you to imagine, begin by feeling the sun kissing your face as you hold a photo or some other representation of your goal.

STEP 6

Start with the End Result

When you use your mind's eye, work on the result you want to achieve and then expand into all the small steps before and afterward. (Don't forget the rewards.)

Mary Lou Retton's goal was to win a gold medal at the Olympics. She wanted it dearly and "saw" it completely. She worked out the writing of her visualization with our colleague and friend Dr. Denis Waitley. She is said to have repeated the visualization ten thousand times. She saw herself relaxed. She told herself, "I have the right to be here." She saw herself go through every motion letter-perfectly. "I see myself coming off the high bars with poised elegance. I see myself throw my arms victoriously into the air. I see Mom with tears of joy streaming down her face. I see the digital scoreboard reading out a perfect ten. I see the audience giving me a tumultuous standing ovation. I see myself getting a contract from Wheaties for three million dollars."

The center of her focus was getting over the bars. But she extended her imagination in both directions until she saw the entire process as clearly as if it were actually happening right before her. Actually doing it was simply repeating something she had already done ten thousand times in her mind.

STEP 7

Conclusion

Closing a visualization should be ritualistic, if it is to be productive. You should use the same closing each time regardless of what you have visualized. The closing should be both relaxing and inspiring. It should uplift us and at the same time truly make clear that we have finished a transcendent experience.

Our recommendation is that you conclude with these words, "And so it is. It cannot be otherwise, and I rejoice because of it. Thank you, God."

4

Affirm Yourself

> **You are where you are because you want to be there. If you want to be somewhere else, you'll change.**

Muhammad Ali was one of the finest boxers in history. But before he received his acclaim, before his name and face became known around the world, he was just another struggling fighter trying to break into the big time.

Perhaps you can remember the day, as we do, when we read the headline on the sports page. There were only three words: "I'm the greatest!"

They were said to the press by a young man named Cassius Clay *before* his first great match with Sonny Liston. At that time, the press scoffed at the upstart. But when he won, they took notice. Not only had he won, but he had *predicted* it.

Clay—later Ali—subsequently went on a world tour constantly reiterating his motto, "I'm the greatest!" But he also began predicting the round in which he would knock out his opponent. In all but one or two cases, he was right!

How could he do that? Had Muhammad Ali tied into some mysterious force that gave him the power to see into the future? Was there something he understood that we didn't?

The answer is yes!

That mysterious force Ali tapped into is called *affirmation*. Affirmations are the words you say to yourself or that others say to you that you believe, think about, and that come about.

Understanding Affirmation

Notice that when Ali spoke, he never said, "I'm great," or "I'm almost the greatest," or even "Next year I'll be the greatest." When he said, simply and clearly, "I'm the greatest!" he was accomplishing three things simultaneously:

First, he was letting his own subconscious know what it had to work with. For the subconscious there is only the present, so he was *defining* himself right then and there. In effect, he was telling his subconscious what it was supposed to believe in the sweet now and now.

Second, by speaking his affirmation out loud and in front of others, he was putting his subconscious on notice that there was no backing down. He had declared it. Now he had to live up to it.

Third, once he had lived up to what he had said by becoming world champion, he got others to believe it as well. Thus, when he said he would put another fighter away in the third round, he made sure that other fighter heard the declaration.

And when the third round came, the other fighter was waiting to be put away. Such was Ali's strength of affirmation that even the other fighter believed it was going to happen. Consequently it did. He psyched himself and other fighters out.

Ali also used other forms of affirmation besides the spoken word. Two of his other techniques were outstaring his opponent during the instructions before the match, and never sitting down in the corner between rounds. These were additional kinesthetic affirmations. They told him and his opponent that he was invincible.

For, you see, while Ali's boxing skills were indeed significant, even greater were his psychological skills. Ali was the ultimate boxer of the mind. All activities need to be won first in the mind and then on the battlefield.

The Importance of Not Making Negative Statements

An affirmation is a statement of belief. Without it, the subconscious is free to be programmed by others as to what to believe. Since the subconscious is untrained, we also know that it believes whatever happens to be poured into it. If it hears negative comments, then it begins to think negatively. If it's told that we're withdrawn, unsure, self-conscious, helpless, it believes that, and we act accordingly.

An excellent example of negative expectations was Mary Decker, in the 1984 Olympics. Mary is an outstanding runner, one of the world's finest. She was supposed to be America's great hope in track. But whenever we heard her on a talk show before the Olympics, in her tone and sometimes in her words, we kept hearing her say, "I'm a jinx, I'm a jinx, I'm a jinx."

We're sure that she wasn't aware of what she was doing. Undoubtedly she was under enormous pressure. But the result was that she was pouring negative statements into her subconscious mind, and it listened. She indeed did seem to be jinxed in the Olympics.

Negative input from the conscious mind results in negative output from the subconscious mind. It's the old law of cause and effect. Cause and effect are one. The problem is that too many of us only see the effects. We only see what the subconscious has wrought. If things go wrong, if we lose, if we fail, we tend to look only at the effect. Most of us never realize that there was a cause of that effect.

If you keep believing what you've been believing, then you'll keep achieving what you've been achieving.

We'd like to repeat a little story we tell in our seminars that touches on this subject. It's about a young monk at a monastery. In this particular order, all the monks were required to take a vow of silence. But at the end of the year each monk was allowed two words that could be spoken to the father.

At the end of the first year, the father asked this new monk what he had to say. The new monk's reply was "Hard bed."

The father nodded and sent the lad on his way.

At the end of the second year, the new monk returned and again was asked what two words he would speak. He replied, "Bad food."

The father nodded and sent him on his way again.

At the end of the third year, when the new monk returned, he spoke up immediately and said, "I quit."

To which the father nodded and said, "No wonder, all you do is complain, complain, complain."

The cause for failure is negative input from the conscious to the subconscious. Be negative consciously and you'll set up your subconscious for negative results. But be positive consciously and you'll set up your subconscious for positive results. It's just that simple.

Belief

> *"Whatever the mind can conceive and believe, the mind can achieve."*
> —DR. NAPOLEON HILL

In order to achieve your goals, you've got to believe you can do it. Just giving lip service won't do. The principle is this: your beliefs determine your actions, and your actions determine your results. Take massive right action and obtain massive right results.

Consciously believing is the key to achieving. But how do we arrive at our beliefs? As noted in the previous two chapters, we first set out a goal in writing. Then we visualize that goal. Finally, we use affirmation to drive home our belief in our abilities to achieve that goal. Affirmation is the key that unlocks the door to belief.

Will Rogers is reported to have said, "I only know what I read in the newspaper." While he may have meant something else, the truth of that statement comes from the fact that we all tend to believe things that are written down.

Another truth is that we all tend to believe something that's been affirmed. Repeated affirmation lends credibility. When we say it out loud, we always have an audience of at least one—our own subconscious mind. And when our subconscious hears us affirming, it at least gives us the benefit of the doubt. It at least says, "Well, he could be right."

When we affirm in front of someone else, we really put the squeeze on our subconscious. It's forced to say, "Wow, you really did it! You committed yourself. If you don't follow through, you'll look the fool and be embarrassed. Now I have to get off my behind and save you on this. I guess I'll have to go to work!"

Can you see the power of affirmation? It forces our subconscious to believe that we really *can*.

How to Affirm

Once we understand the vital importance of affirming in achieving our future greatness and living up to our potential, our next question must be, "How do we affirm?"

In our seminars we suggest that people use the following technique. As you read this book, we suggest you follow it yourself. At first you may want to do it alone until you get the hang of it. Later on, you'll probably feel comfortable doing it in public.

1. The first thing you must do is stand. Standing brings your full consciousness to attention. We always suggest that people stand whenever they're doing something important— for example, making a phone call. The next time you're making a phone call, instead of sitting down, stand up and listen to yourself. You'll be amazed at your increased energy, brilliance, newfound enthusiasm and power. You'll dazzle the people on the other end of the line with your heightened energy level.

2. When you're affirming, take your index finger and the center finger of your hand and jab yourself in the center of your chest. This engages the sense of touch and feeling. The index finger is the most sensitive instrument of touch in our bodies. It is the portal to our mind. What the index finger touches, we "see." The middle finger adds strength to the index finger. When we jab both of these into our chests, our minds know instantly that we're talking about ourselves, and there can be no doubt. We engage our full attention by doing this.

3. Finally, as you jab yourself in the chest, make a state-

ment of affirmation. Make it loud and clear and be sure that your voice isn't quavering. *Mean it!*

In the *Star Wars* sequel, *The Empire Strikes Back,* Yoda, the Jedi teacher, tries to implant into Luke Skywalker the means of engaging the "force" that is the greatest power in the universe. He says to his pupil, "Luke, there is no *try.* There is either do or not do." The "force" is the felt power of affirmation. You make it so by saying it is so.

In those simple words is a world of meaning. When you say something such as "I'm going to *try* to be the greatest," or "I'm going to *try* to be beautiful," or "I'm going to *try* to succeed," remember that it doesn't cost any more to affirm greatness than it does to affirm mediocrity. So why affirm anything less?

Affirmations don't have to be fancy, long or drawn-out. Simplicity is the key. And they should be in the present, not the future tense (remember, the subconscious doesn't operate in the future, it only has now!).

Your affirmation should be spoken with as much *conviction* as you can give it. If you find yourself stumbling over the words, start over. A hint here is that if you just can't make yourself say it, *shout* it. Go for loudness. Blow the lid off. You'll get the message across to your subconscious.

Do It Often

The more you affirm, the sooner you'll put your obedient subconscious to work and get results. You master your mind; don't let it master you.

> *Touch yourself and say, "I've got greatness in me. I am a genius and I am applying my genius."*

According to Indian thought, once we state something ten thousand times it becomes a mantra, a frequently repeated thought form that molds and shapes our future. When you affirm regularly, you'll find yourself tuning in to the depth of your being and eavesdropping on yourself and your future. We affirmed we'd sell 1.5 million copies of our book *Chicken Soup for the Soul,* using a technique called "by-pass marketing," and now we're doing it.

Your inner knower—the part of your subconscious that gets things done—will start parroting back your affirmation, saying, "You're the greatest!" Repeated affirmations will eventually block and edit out the counterproductive, negative and self-sabotaging old thoughts.

What to Affirm

Thus far we've talked about how and when to affirm. The next logical step is to ask ourselves, "What should I affirm?"

This is, of course, a personal choice. It really depends on your purpose and your goals. We suggest that you have a main affirmation that you constantly repeat as well as other affirmations that you use as needed.

> *Touch yourself and say, "I've got great talent. I am using it all for my highest good, now!"*

You'll need to create your own main self-affirmation. Go for something that's simple, positive, succinct and constructive. It should be easy to repeat, so that it becomes like a perpetual continuous-loop tape recording in the mind.

It's a good idea to have an affirmation that you feel comfortable with first thing in the morning. When you get out of bed and stumble to the mirror, that first look can be disconcerting, if you're like most of us. Hair disheveled, no makeup, growth of beard, sleep-wrinkled where the pillow or sheet made impressions on our face. The most obvious reaction is to say, "Aaaauuugh!"

If we succumb to what's most obvious, what are we telling the subconscious? Aren't we inputting the information that we are somehow terrible? Aren't we giving ourselves negative input? How is that negative input going to affect us for the rest of the day? What are the results we're going to achieve? Is the subconscious going to be all gears forward trying to get positive results? Or is it instead going to work to live up to that cry of dismay?

> **Touch yourself and say, "I have great visions and I'm making them real."**

There is an alternative. When we get up, what if we stare at ourselves in the mirror and instead smile and say something like, "You know, you're *okay*." Or even, "You're great." It isn't hard to do.

Right now, as you're reading this, stop for just a moment and smile. Take a deep, relaxing breath and just smile. Notice how it changes your whole feeling state. Don't wait for someone or something to make you happy. Choose to be happy right now. It is a choice, and one of the oldest techniques known is simply to choose to smile.

Start each day with a smile. Start by smiling at yourself in the mirror. Say, "Good morning. I love you. We're going to have a great day today."

And then follow through. Go forward into your day with the knowledge and belief that you are going to produce great results.

The real question to ask ourselves is "What am I saying to myself about myself?"

Am I talking myself up? Am I my own best cheerleader? Don't forget, the first person you must impress every day before you go out is *you*. If you're impressed, the world will be impressed.

Multimillionaire W. Clement Stone, owner of the Aeon Corporation in Chicago, says that he requires his staff to say each morning, "I feel great, I feel healthy, I feel terrific." He has trained hundreds of thousands of his salespeople to use those three self-motivating affirmations to achieve greatness and financial success.

Another great place to affirm ourselves is in the shower. We all sing in the shower sometimes. In addition to singing, why not hug ourselves and tell the various parts of our body how wonderful they are? For example, talk health into every organ in your body. Say, "Mind, you are marvelous. Mind, you have profitable ideas that work easily and effortlessly." Nobody's going to see. Nobody but our subconscious is going to know. It can be a private and personal booster session. Touch your hair and say, "What terrific hair!" Touch your face and say, "My face is beautiful." When you come out of the shower, you'll be roaring like a lion.

Does It Really Work?

Of course it does! Dr. Wayne Dyer, who has written many successful books but is probably best known for *Your Erroneous Zones*, told his colleagues at St. John's University, long before he was published, "I am going to be a best-selling author." They laughed. But to date he has sold more than 58 million books.

> *Touch yourself and say, "I see it. I feel it. I believe it. And then I take action toward my evolving prosperity!"*

The best coaches in the world, like Lou Holtz of Notre Dame fame in Indiana, always call their athletes "Champ." Why? Is it because the athlete is indeed a champ? Certainly not at first. But coaches know that what the conscious mind hears, the subconscious will act upon. Lou Holtz takes losing teams and within two years has number one winning teams.

> *Touch yourself and say, "I am a big-time winner!"*

Affirm Your Goals

Affirmation works not just on our overall personality, but on our specific goals as well. Wayne Gretsky, for example, at the age of seventeen, was a superior athlete. He had the opportunity to play two different sports—hockey or soccer. He loved hockey.

When he tried out for professional hockey, he was told, "You only weigh 172 pounds. You're too light. The average player weighs in excess of 226 pounds. You won't be able to survive out there."

> *Touch yourself and say, "I feel really healthy!"*

Gretsky reportedly simply affirmed, "I go where the hockey puck's going."

He was totally committed to the sport. Today he has a multi-million-dollar hockey contract and endorsements that pay him in the millions. He has been voted MVP (most valuable player) seven times in a row. His affirmation was simple and clear-cut. It led him to big-time winnings within his chosen sport.

Affirm Others

It costs nothing to do, yet it pays dividends that are profound. When you affirm another human being, you raise his or her self-esteem. The other person, in turn, will reciprocate, and you will receive bountiful rewards. If you're sincere, it's the simplest and most effective way of favorably influencing others.

There are three kinds of affirmations or compliments that we can give to others. The first is to affirm someone's physical attributes. This is historically how most men have complimented women. The second way is to affirm mental virtues. These affirmations go to the intellectual giant in our class, to someone who has done well academically or in business.

These two ways are generally limited. We can't compliment *everyone* on their mental virtues or their physical attributes, or else we would rightly be accused of being insincere. But there is a third way we can affirm others, and that is for their qualities, their achievements and their actions.

Everyone has a set of core qualities that they express. They are funny, sincere, courageous, disciplined, well-organized, loving, compassionate, dedicated, or persistent. Perhaps they demonstrate high levels of integrity, morality, ethics or honesty. Maybe they are straightforward, a risk taker or someone who cares deeply about animals or children. When we affirm these qualities in someone, we are acknowledging them at a core level. This is the deepest and most powerful kind of affirmation we can give another person.

A person has succeeded at a project, a child has learned how to ride a bike, a friend is a skier. We can affirm all of these people for their accomplishments, thereby adding to their self-esteem.

Affirm everyone you meet. Say something nice to them. It will help them immensely in their lives, and it will come back to you in many positive and often unseen ways.

> *Touch yourself and say, "I am an important person and I feel totally great!"*

Results

Through affirmation—and, of course, writing down our goals and using the power of visualization—we can achieve amazing results. Just how amazing really depends on each of us individually. But here are just a few things you can be by using this technique:

I am Prosperous now.
I am Happy now.
I am Healthy now.
I am Loving, Loved and Beloved now.
I am Beautiful now.
I am Joyous now.
I am Peaceful now.
I am Successful now.
I am Rich now.
I am Self-Confident now.
I am Friendly now.

Affirmations and the other techniques we've mentioned allow us to change our beliefs, assumptions and opinions about that most important person—ourselves. They allow us to harness those 18 billion brain cells and get them all going in a singular and purposeful direction. The subconscious is engaged in a process that transforms us. It's invisible. It doesn't hurt. It doesn't take a long time. It just happens.

Touch yourself and say, "I am one terrific person!"

Once you become accustomed to the process and its elementary mechanics, you'll be able to do it with increasing frequency and facility.

Let's say that your belief about yourself is that you are unattractive and have difficulty making friends. You believe that others don't like you.

Key #1

Start the change process by setting a goal. The goal is to be loved and cherished by others. Or it may be to find someone with whom to have a romantic relationship. Write down your goal, and make it as crystal-clear as you can both in your mind and in your writing of it.

Key #2

Visualize the goal as completed. Use the seven steps to visualization that we gave you in the last chapter. "See" yourself as the person you want to be. Perhaps you've seen an actor or actress do something that you saw as warm, friendly and loving. You can become that actor or actress in your mind. "See" yourself in the appropriate setting. Perhaps you're in Hawaii with someone you love. Everyone is friendly, delighted to talk with you. In fact, you have so many friends that you have to excuse yourself from one to take up a conversation with another. They all fawn over you, draw you out, seek your attention, advice and wise counsel. Add in the auditory and kinesthetic dimensions to deepen the impact.

Hear the words and sounds you would hear. If you're in Hawaii, hear the sound of the surf, the Hawaiian music and the words of conversation. And then create the feelings you think you would feel if all of that were happening right now. Feel those feelings all through your body. Fantastic!

Key #3

Affirm the desired results. Before you go to sleep, you could "play back" a series of affirmations:

I am lively.
I am outgoing.
I am friendly.
I am poised.
I am charming.
I am meeting people who are attracted to me.
I am lovely.

Repeat these affirmations every night before you go to sleep and let them soothe you as if they were waves gently caressing a beach. Practice them for a month until they become automatic, until you've woven them into the fabric of your being. Now they will automatically repeat themselves to you throughout the day. They will become like a popular song that you've heard on the radio. They'll be inside your mind.

By the time this happens, you'll be far along the path to becoming the person you want to be. Your subconscious will get the message, and it will be reflected in every action you take, producing the desired responses in others. You will become the self you desire.

Affirmation works. In fact, it may be the most powerful force in the universe. Just as Muhammad Ali used it to accomplish amazing results, as others have used it, so, too, can you.

Life Is a Balancing Act

"I am an artist at living—my work of art is my life."
—SUZUKI

Imagine a tightrope walker in a circus. He is on a rope suspended a few feet above the straw-covered floor. His purpose is to walk the rope from one end to the other. He holds a long bar in his hands to help him maintain his balance. But he must do more than simply walk. On his shoulders he balances a chair. And in that chair sits a young woman who is herself balancing a rod on her forehead, and on top of that rod a plate.

The tightrope artist doesn't begin until all the elements above him are aligned. Only then does he move forward, carefully, slowly, across the rope.

If at any time one of the items should start to drift off balance, he must stop until he can get all of them in perfect alignment again. For the tightrope artist, balance is everything. Should his balance fail him, he will surely fall.

Life on a Tightrope

We suggest that life is very much a balancing act and that we are always just a step away from a fall. We are constantly trying to move forward with our purpose, to achieve our goals, all the while trying to keep in balance the various elements of our lives.

Getting Out of Balance

Many of us get out of balance with regard to money. If we don't have sufficient money, then our lives become a money chase. We constantly devote our energies toward improving our finances. In the process we tend to take energy away from our families, our mates, our spiritual and mental needs, even our health. More important, we don't move forward toward our life purposes. We don't proceed along the tightrope. We think that only when we get our finances straightened out can we devote our energies to all the other aspects of our lives and then proceed with our purposes.

Other areas of our lives could be out of harmony. It could be a relationship with a wife or husband. It could be a spiritual emptiness that is gnawing at our insides. It could be lack of appropriate social contact. It could be illness. If any aspect of our lives draws a disproportionate amount of energy, we have to shortchange the other aspects. This throws us off, and we are unable to more forward on life's tightrope until a balance can be reestablished.

Getting in Balance

Our first priority, therefore, is getting our life in balance. We need to deal with any areas that are taking too much energy and put them in perspective, align them so that we have energy available for all areas.

We need to create a balance of winning identities as father or mother, lover, husband or wife, son or daughter, worker, participant, finisher and so forth. Only when each identity is fulfilled will that area be functioning and not overdrawing our energy.

But it doesn't happen by itself. Achieving a balanced life is a choice that each of us continually makes second by second, thought by thought, feeling by feeling. On the one hand, we can simply exist. But on the other, we can choose to pack our seconds and create valuable minutes in all aspects of our lives.

It's important here to understand that others cannot do this for us. Only we can be us and only you, you. No one can think, breathe, feel, see, experience, love or die for any of us. Inside, we are what we are. We all come into life without a map, an operating manual or a definition of ourselves, other than male or female. It's up to us to discover who we are and who we can be. It's up to us to balance all the different aspects of our lives. We can do it by pushing the "decide" button in our lives.

Making an Assessment

At first it's important to stop and assess how we're doing. We should look at all the various aspects of our lives that we are constantly juggling, constantly trying to keep in balance. These include:

Marriage and family
Finances
Health and physical fitness
Social contact
Emotional growth

Spiritual development
Mental growth

Are we able to devote ample energy to all areas? Or are we tipped off to one side, unbalanced in one direction?

Making It Happen

To us, an example of a person who has worked hard his whole life to get his life in balance is Sylvester Stallone. He is a magnificent example of a man who learned to balance on a tightrope.

As a child, Stallone grew up a loner, hyperkinetic and emotionally tormented. He was in and out of several schools. At Drexel University he was tested and told that his future calling was as an elevator repairman! His father frequently beat him up, telling him he was no good and advising him to develop his body because he didn't have any brains—a line he used later in *Rocky*.

When he decided on acting, his life was out of balance in many respects, from financial to emotional. And these imbalances resulted in early failure. Early in his acting career, he suffered failure after failure. But he worked at learning. In a magazine article Mark read, Sly said: "If I'd succeeded right away in acting, I wouldn't have sought out writing. Eventually writing became more interesting to me than acting. You see, success is usually the culmination of controlling failure. Through my failure I found different ways to reverse my problems and get into the mainstream of Hollywood. If I'd made it right away as an actor, I would have stopped at a certain level and stayed there, probably as a character actor."

Over a period of years, Stallone learned how to balance the emotional, physical and mental aspects of his life. Then one night he watched Muhammad Ali fight Chuck Wepner and heard the thrill of the crowd watching the underdog go the distance. Deeply inspired, he wrote the script for Rocky in only three-and-a-half days. He then told producers that the script was only for sale with him as the lead. And early on, most producers turned him down. The rest is history. Rocky grossed more than $100 million.

With Stallone's finances assured, he still had imbalance in his life. He didn't feel sufficient love in his life and went through a divorce. He built his body from being in good shape to being in peak shape. He developed his mind and developed his spiritual beliefs.

His personal transformation took him many years, but it eventually resulted in a balance that has brought him unparalleled success. Today he has a long-term contract offering him $20 million a picture plus a percentage of the profits. Stallone is a living example of what bringing balance to an out-of-balance life can do.

This is the shortest chapter in this book, but probably the most important. It says succinctly what we consider to be the ultimate message. What remains is figuring out just what is out of balance and how to put it into alignment. That's what we'll cover in the remaining chapters.

You Can Do It with Love

"Life's a banquet, and most poor suckers are starving to death!"

—AUNTIE MAME

The absence of love is one of the most frightening things that can happen to a human being. Withdraw love and you can crush an otherwise happy, healthy person.

We all need love to survive, and we need it from our earliest days. Countless studies have shown that human (and other animal) babies need to be held, cuddled, caressed and otherwise loved from the moment of birth. With that love they grow and mature into healthy adults. Without that love they sicken mentally, physically and spiritually, and in extreme cases even die.

There's some indication that the need for love is so universal that it applies to the plant kingdom as well. Studies at the

University of Iowa showed that plants responded and grew better when loving words were continuously spoken to them.

Self-Esteem

The need for love doesn't diminish as we grow into adults. If
anything, the need increases, for love becomes tied to self-
esteem, how you esteem yourself from the inside out. If all the
world's a stage, and actors mimic our true feelings, consider
what happens when an audience boos or hisses a performance.
The actors and actresses withdraw and say, "They hated me!"
But if the audience is warm and receptive, if it gives the performers a loud ovation, the same actors and actresses are
likely to say, "They loved me!"

Beyond money or glory, actors and actresses perform for the
love of the audience. Bob Hope, at ninety-plus years old, is a
perfect example of someone who keeps performing for the love
of his audience. He has had vast wealth since the Depression.
Beyond money or glory, we, too, perform for the love of others.
In fact, we need it.

> *If you're into love, you haven't got time for any-
> thing else.*

Love tells us that we're worthwhile. It feeds our self-esteem
and our self-confidence. When we know we are loved, we can
outperform ourselves. If we suspect that we aren't loved, our
performance can plummet.

A businessperson may be a peak performer because he or
she believes that there is a loving, supportive spouse at home.
But if that businessperson learns suddenly that the love
counted on isn't there, his or her ability to maintain a high
work level may be substantially diminished.

Consider the case of a financially successful husband who discovers that his wife is leaving him. He hadn't realized he was taking her love for granted. He had thought his work in the business world was sufficient to protect and reward that love.

Suddenly it is withdrawn. Without love, he can't sleep, he can't eat, he can't think, he can't perform at work. The sudden withdrawal of love is a shock to the body and mind and keeps him from functioning.

To maintain peak performance, we need peak love. We need to be reassured daily that we are loved. Love builds our perception of our own value. It increases our self-esteem.

> *"Everyone has two choices. We're either full of love . . . or full of fear."*
>
> **—ALBERT EINSTEIN**

Takers

Because love is so universally necessary, there are some people who try to take it. They demand it from others without offering it in return. We're sure you know the kind of people we're talking about. Perhaps they say to us, "Why haven't you called me? I've been waiting for your phone call." These people want the loving feeling that comes from knowing that another person wants/needs to talk to them.

We're sure you've also met the kind of person who hogs a conversation. We begin a conversation on mutual ground with each of us alternately sharing and listening. But slowly this person begins dominating the conversation with repeated stories of how marvelous his or her work is or how wonderful his or her children are or how terrific his or her expensive new car is. Very quickly we are boxed out as the other person, intoxicated with himself or herself, drones on, only occasionally glancing at us to be sure that we appreciate his or her grandeur.

These sad people have such low self-esteem that they must

command us to admire them. The more we're put off by their tactics, the more frightened they become that we're withdrawing love, so they push harder. Ultimately they push so hard that no one can stand to be their friend.

Not getting enough love leads to suffering. Neurotic behavior, even mental illness, frequently results from a lack of love. Studies have shown that as much as 87 percent of *physical* illness is caused by not getting or experiencing enough love.

When we don't have love, our judgment wavers. We become incompetent and incapable. We turn inward, and as our self-esteem and self-confidence shrink, our fears grow. Ultimately, the loss of love can lead to a catatonic state.

The only remedy is more love. To get more love coming in, we individually need to stimulate the process by putting more love out.

Givers

Getting love is really so simple that it's positively amazing that everyone isn't awash in a surplus of it. There are millions and millions of people out there waiting to love us. It's all out there for the asking. We just have to know how to phrase the question.

The way to get love is to give it. Life gives to the giver and takes from the taker.

> *A lost opportunity to give love is a lost opportunity to receive love.*

If you ever feel a lack of love, if you feel that you're not getting enough love, then give yourself away. As soon as you give yourself away, you will be flooded with love.

Jack recently received a card from a person who had heard him speak. It read, "The love I give you is secondhand because I have already experienced it first."

People ask us, "How do I 'give myself away'?"

One of the best ways to do this is to go to a convalescent home. This is especially true for men. Men walking into a convalescent home are often taken aback by seeing other men sitting there unable to move, victims of stroke.

Just walk into that home, check in at the desk and then go right up to one of the people and say, "I'm an official hugger around here. I just came in to create good feelings. I'd like to share a hug with you, and if you need my support, I'm here to help you in any way I can."

If you're coming from the heart, these older people will respond to you.

Often after sitting and talking with the old folks for a while, when you get ready to leave, they'll reach out and kiss your hand. You'll see tears forming in their eyes and rolling down their cheeks.

You will make them feel loved and, at least for that moment, vital and alive. Seeing and realizing this will really revitalize *you*, too, because you'll know intuitively that you are loved in return. You'll "see" that you are a worthwhile person. You'll realize that by giving yourself away, you will improve your own self-esteem.

Mother Teresa is the world's best example of someone who supplies simple acts of kindness like holding hands, hugging and making others comfortable in their grief, sickness and times of trouble.

Loving Techniques

As we've seen, love is necessary to our well-being. It supports and promotes. It keeps us afloat. It gives us the confidence to grow. Love, in fact, is growth food. Regardless of the goals we may have set for ourselves, regardless of what our purpose may be, unless and until we have enough love, we will find that things don't work out for us. Only when our love needs are met will the rest of our life come into balance.

Christ said, "The kingdom of heaven is within." That includes love. Love is an inside job.

We've also seen that the way to receive love is to give it unconditionally, without expecting something in return. The more you give it away, the more it will come back to you. The more you love, the more you will be loved.

To help us get the love we want, need and deserve, we have developed seven loving techniques. We guarantee these will bring you the love you are looking for.

Loving Technique #1: Hugging

We advocate hugging. Mark and his wife, Patty, conducted a national "hug survey" and discovered that 83 percent of us grew up getting less than one hug a day. Even if we won't admit it, 99 percent of us want more hugs than we've been getting. A hug is a perfect way of immediately giving and receiving love from another human being.

At their self-esteem institute in Cincinnati, Ohio, Drs. Bill and Dean McGrane found that people need several hugs a day just to be psychologically "balanced." The minimum, they say, is four hugs, just for maintenance, and the requirement for growth is twelve hugs!

Overcoming the Hugging Taboo

The problem with hugging, however, is that in our culture physical contact between people who barely know each other is considered taboo, particularly when it's between men. Even though a hug is a nonsexual statement, it's still considered off-limits by some people.

The taboo notwithstanding, whenever we give our seminars we always encourage the members of our audiences to hug one another several times during the talk. Mark can remember one such time when he was in Calgary, Canada, talking to about five hundred people, mostly men. He said, "If you're not stuck in your macho-ism, I'd love to hug all of you when this is over."

Afterward, he was out in the hallway hugging away. One guy who must have been six-and-a-half feet tall was working his way down the hall. Mark grabbed him in a hug and asked, "Are you into hugging?" He looked surprised, and Mark realized he was simply on his way out and had had no intention of being hugged. Then he said, "Before you did that, I wasn't into hugging. Now I think I am!"

Hugging is something that we can all respond to, once we get past the taboo. The experience usually surprises most people. The fact that everyone at a seminar is doing it takes the pressure off it, at least for the moment. The intimacy it instantly creates is warm and pleasant. Suddenly people who would otherwise never hug realize that they really do like giving and receiving this form of love.

> *In our advanced society, we need high touch to balance the high tech.*

How to Hug Properly

Everyone knows how to hug, correct? So how could there be a right way and a wrong way to do it? Any hug is, of course, better than no hug at all. But some hugs are better than others. Some people know how to really get into their hugs, to give and get the most. You can, too, with a minimal amount of practice.

1. When you're hugging someone shorter than you, bend your knees. Get shorter. It's a sign of courtesy and consideration to do so. It also prevents the short person from getting whiplash.

    Remember to hug little children at their level, squat down to their size and hug them. Research shows that little boys only get one sixth the hugs little girls get. Don't discriminate against little boys; generously hug them too—they need it. And if the situation presents itself, hug someone in a wheelchair. They are often neglected and forgotten.

2. When you're in the hug, open your heart. Give the hug all you've got from the heart (in India it's called the "heart chakra," your love-energy zone) and really lavish your recipient with love.

    Think of the hug as the key that opens the pathway to the heart. Psychiatrist Jerry Jampolski, author of *Love Is Letting Go of Fear*, and head of the Center for Attitudinal Healing in Tiburon, California, teaches dying children to open their hearts and heal one another. The opening of the heart is another way of saying that we are giving away our love, giving away ourselves. And in so doing we receive.

3. After the physical hug, give an "eye hug." Look deeply and penetratingly into the eyes of the person you just hugged. Silently, and inside yourself, say, "Thank you and I love you," if this is an appropriate feeling for you. If not, say something that is appropriate for you.

    Few people make good eye contact. Dare to be different by maintaining magnificent eye contact. Really touch the spirit of the eyes you embrace. Look with what we call soft eyes, the eyes of acceptance and love. Practice soft eyes the next time you look at someone. You can feel the difference. Notice the response it creates.

"Arms are for hugging."
—FROM A BUMPER STICKER

Learning these techniques for hugging will make it more rewarding for you. The more you hug, the more your self-esteem will grow, and you'll have new levels of awareness of how important hugging is to human life and love.

Great Huggers

As an art form, hugging has many artists, especially those who have practiced and perfected the techniques. Our friend Dr. Leo Buscaglia, author of *Living, Loving and Learning,* is a master hugger. Leo is in the *Guinness Book of World Records* for being the world's greatest hugger. After one of his seminars, he often stands ready to hug, love, care, listen to and share with everyone who wants to touch him. Sometimes this touching process can last up to six hours! People wait because they are hug-deprived and he has focused their minds on the need for hugs.

Mothers are great huggers. They can hug and love their children until it makes the kids feel absolutely wonderful. What are we all, if not grown-up kids? The kind of hugs that Mama gave are needed just as much now as they were when we were children.

Family Hugging

Remember to embrace daily the family members who live in close proximity to you. Explain to them that you are involved in a hugging experiment and you'd like them to be your co-hugging experimenter for the next thirty days. At the end of thirty days you and they will hug forever.

Research has shown that hugging has positive effects on children's language development and IQ. It causes measurable changes in the hugger and huggee and has healing and therapeutic benefits.

Dare to Hug

Intuitively we all know that hugging feels good, dispels loneliness and overcomes fears. Therefore, it stands to reason that we should hug *everyone*, not just our best friends. (I still remember one lady who told me, "I can't believe it, but I actually hugged the person I dislike most intensely!")

Remember that hugging is *nonsexual*. You aren't making a sexual statement when you hug another person. You're making a statement about human love. Love/hug statements have a long tradition. Mark's Scandinavian forefathers used the Norse word *hugga*, which meant to comfort, hold close and console.

Ask permission before you give a hug. Some people have been severely sexually and physically abused as children or as adults and may find hugging others a bit overwhelming or overstimulating in terms of their emotions, so it's always best to ask first. Ninety-nine percent of people will say yes if you ask.

So dare to hug. Go for twelve hugs a day. Often while we are walking through airports, two or more of our students will pull us off into an instant group hug. It's joyous and wonderful.

Dare to request a hug when you need one. The most aware parents, seeing a child in need of reassurance, take the initiative and say, "I need a hug." The child now willingly gives and, even more importantly, receives. This mentally and emotionally refreshes and reinforces the young ones to move forward openly.

Love Notes

We always advocate sending love notes. It both surprises and thrills the recipient. It's an excellent way for us to send love to another. When people receive them, they feel so warm and loved that they can hardly wait to get back to us to return that love.

Love notes allow our love to flow even when we aren't present. They create a special feeling when the person realizes that we cared enough to take the time to write.

When to Send Love Notes

Send them any and every time you can. An excellent time to send a love note is if you're helping someone to pack. Hide the love note in a pocket, a purse, a wallet, or a shoe. Put it somewhere that will surprise the recipient.

A woman at one of our seminars told about this humorous and novel way to send a love note. She had dictated the grocery shopping list to her husband. When he was finished writing, she took the list and went shopping.

There were fourteen items on the list, and when she came to number thirteen, she saw that her husband had written in "Sex!"

She said it caught her so off guard, she just about fell apart laughing. The store manager came over and said, "Is there anything we can help you with?"

She said, "No, my husband's already promised that!"

One parent we know leaves a three-by-five yellow Post-it note with a love note for her fourteen-year-old daughter every day. She might put it on the bathroom mirror for her to find in the morning. Sometimes she puts the note in her lunch box or on one of her school books. She writes one every day.

They say things like, "I love your sense of humor." "Thanks for helping me with the dog last night. You made my job a lot easier." Or, "I am so glad you were born. Every time I think of you, I smile inside my heart."

One day the parent went into her daughter's room looking for her hair dryer, which she found there. On her way out of the room, she saw that her daughter had placed about fifty of her favorite messages on the back of her door. Every time she went to leave her room, her daughter was visually reminded of how much she was loved and appreciated. What a wonderful technique. Why don't you start to use it tonight!

As a bonus, save your love notes and letters, and someday, upon reviewing them, you will cherish the memories they evoke.

Important Love Notes

Some love notes can be vitally important. These are the ones sent to people who are often deprived of love—teachers who served us well, those who are incarcerated or away with the armed forces or, even more dramatically today, older parents or grandparents, left alone trying to care for themselves in the twilight of their years.

These people usually die at home, and while the death certificate may list a specific disease, almost uniformly they die of a broken heart.

Most of their friends may have passed on, and they have few connections left with the world around them. They may wake up in the middle of the night feeling alienated, shut down and turned off. They feel tuned out of life, as if nobody really cares about them anymore.

It's at times like this that they take out the letter we sent a month earlier that's already been reread twenty or thirty times.

They look again at the letter that tells them what we've been doing, what the grandchildren are up to, when we're planning to come and visit next, even if it's six months away—a letter that tells them how much we love them. It's this letter that gets them through the night and on into the next day. The letters we have seen are often tearstained, tattered and taped together from frequent rereading, pondering, cherishing.

We always ask people to write a love note to their parents, if they're fortunate enough to still have their parents with them. If not, write to another relative or older person who has been supportive in the past. We don't have to worry about punctuation, grammar, spelling or syntax. The reader doesn't care. We just need to write from our hearts to theirs. They'll know what we mean. Love has two aspects—givingness and forgiveness. John Bradshaw teaches that forgiveness is tough-love in manifestation. Write both kinds of love letters to mend your own heart and feelings.

It doesn't take long to write the note. What we're asking for is perhaps two or three minutes out of a twenty-four-hour day. It takes so little for us to give this note of love, yet it will be so appreciated, and ultimately we will receive so much back from it.

Not long ago Mark was sitting in a Jacuzzi with his wife, and she said to him, "I've heard you say dozens of times to write a love note to the folks. Well, yesterday I did it." With his wife's and his mother-in-law's permission, here is just one paragraph from this "four-handkerchief" love note, which says better than we can just what we're talking about.

Dear Mom:
I just want to tell you that I love you. More important than that, I want to tell you my earliest recollection of loving you. I remember waking up one day when I was only three years old. The bed was big and I was little. I slid out and I remember walking toward the kitchen fol-

lowing the aromas of the pancakes and other foods you were making. And I saw you standing there and I just knew that I loved you so much.

Love,
Patty

Cuddling

We are both into cuddling with our wives. We both fly a quarter-million miles a year giving seminars around the world, and about a third of the time our wives fly with us. When we are on the plane we cuddle each other.

It really doesn't make any difference where you are. Cuddling is a warm and affectionate way of giving and receiving love. Sometimes it will even bring you unexpected rewards. Occasionally when we're on the plane with our wives, a stewardess will ask if we're newly married, to which we usually answer, "Yes." (We always feel as if we've just been married.) As a result we often get a free bottle of champagne! What a fun bonus!

> *"If you have enough love, you'll be the happiest and most powerful person in the world."*
> **—DR. EMMET FOX**

If you don't have another person to cuddle, try cuddling a teddy bear. If you feel that's too childish, something an adult should never do, let us refer you to the last episode of "M*A*S*H." It was the most watched of any episode of any series in history. In it, Radar O'Reilly cuddles his teddy bear. The others all wanted to take it away from him. They said, "Look, you're an adult. You're too big to have a little blankie."

But Radar knew better. He needed to give (and receive) love, and there was no other opportunity where he was. So for him the teddy bear was vital, regardless of his age.

In some of our longer weekend seminars, we'll bring ten or

twenty teddy bears. It is amazing, but by Sunday, they'll all be in use, with someone holding each one.

Say "I Love You"

Because love implies sex in our society, we can't often walk right up to another person and say, "I love you." They may wonder at our motives and as a result perhaps give us a quick brush-off. But there are a lot of other ways of saying "I love you" to another person.

One excellent method is to be tender and affectionate in what we say. Those who have taken a Dale Carnegie course know he always recommends that we say something positive before we break any bad news. The idea is that the positive comment comes from love, and the other person will know that we aren't attacking them, aren't trying to hurt them, even when we have to give them bad news or corrective feedback.

Which reminds us of a joke about this very same subject. After hearing the admonition to say something positive before breaking bad news, one woman determined to put it into practice. She and her husband had two beautiful sons. One day something terrible happened and she called her husband. She began, "Dear, you know our two beautiful sons?"

Of course he replied in the affirmative, wondering what she was getting at. She continued, "Well, one of them *didn't* fall out of a tree and break his arm!"

Speak with Love

When we're tender and affectionate in the way we talk to other human beings, whether they're strangers or closely related to us, we are offering them love. Unfortunately, this is often the exception rather than the rule.

Because we travel so much, we eat about two-thirds of our

meals in restaurants. In so doing, we can't help but watch
other people's behavior.

Frequently we see two obviously married people eating together. Because they have chosen to be married to each other,
you would assume that regardless of the length of their relationship, they would have love in their eyes, in their move-
ments and in their words.

Instead of that, we often see people abusing each other with
harsh words and comments. Their words are like knives jab-
bing at one another. Their relationship has turned from loving
to adversarial. We can't help but think that all it would take
to change everything would be a few loving comments. Just
the words "I love you" might be enough to rekindle the love
that once must have shone between them.

We are known to others, perhaps more than anything else,
by the words we speak. If the words are tactfully honest and
filled with love, others will listen, will grow and will return our
love in multiples of what we've given.

> **Life treats you as you treat life.**

Having a very positive attitude when we speak with others
can reap rewards that we may be totally unaware of at the
time. This fact was driven home to us by a very good friend of
ours, Al Sizer. Al, who lives in Portland, Oregon, decided one
Friday morning that he had had a very good week in business
and wanted to reward himself. (We encourage you to reward
yourself immediately for anything you feel you've done particularly well.)

In Portland they have an excellent restaurant called
Daisy's. Al decided to go there, but by the time he arrived,
the line for tables was already half a block long, so he sat at
the counter.

Sitting next to him was a taciturn man who was acting very withdrawn and apparently didn't want to be disturbed. Al has a wonderfully effervescent, boyish quality. He began talking to this fellow and finally broke through his shell. They ate together for almost two hours. Then Al realized the time and said that he had appointments. He gave the man his card and got one in return, never expecting to see him again.

On Wednesday of the next week, the same man came to Al's office with tears in his eyes, saying that Al had saved his life. Of course, Al was flabbergasted. Then the fellow poured out his story.

It turned out that on the morning they had breakfast together, the man had just come from his doctor, who told him that X rays showed he had a terminal illness, one that would prove to be excruciatingly painful toward the end. On the spot, the fellow had decided to commit suicide. But before doing that, he had decided to have one last great meal and he went to Daisy's. There he ran into Al, who spoke to him so affectionately and so affirmatively that he decided not to end his own life and thus deprive his wife and children of the few months left to him.

This very Wednesday morning, however, he had gone back to the doctor to learn that somehow the X rays had been switched. He had an impacted colon, not a life-threatening illness at all. He was crying because if Al hadn't been there, by then he would have been dead.

We never know what a kind word will mean to another person.

Act with Love

We all know that actions speak louder than words. If we tell someone, "I love you," either in those words or others, and then we do something to indicate that we don't really mean it, our actions will reveal us. That's why, in all things, it's important to act the same as we speak.

The perfect illustration for this, we feel, is a true story that happened many years ago involving Andrew Carnegie, one of the country's first and greatest millionaires and philanthropists.

It was in New York on a rainy day that a disheveled old lady came into a department store to get out of the rain and ask for some help. However, because she was dripping wet and appeared to be penniless, no one would bother with her.

Except for one salesman, a young man who said, "Would you like a chair while you wait for someone to come and pick you up?" And he arranged a taxi for her. Before she left she said, "Young man, please write down your name and address on a piece of paper and give it to me." And he did.

The next day Andrew Carnegie, this woman's son, called up the store and said that he wanted to buy all the furniture to outfit a Scottish castle he had just bought. He said further that he wanted this one salesman, the same young man, to do all the selling and get all the commission. In addition, he wanted the young man to accompany him to Scotland to help install it.

The manager concealed his shock and said that the young man was inexperienced and that he himself had worked there for years and would be happy to take on this sizable task.

To which Carnegie replied, "My mother said this young man showed kindness to her even though he didn't know who she was. That tells me that he understands people and business. He gets the assignment, and I want him to get all the commission. I'll check back to see if he did, and if he didn't, I'll take my future business elsewhere."

> **Love is the only thing in the world that you have to give away to get.**

By acting with kindness, the young man was showing human love. The rewards came back to him in multiples. How we act is how others perceive us. If we act with love, we will receive love in abundance in return.

Smile

Another marvelous and easy method of giving ourselves away is to smile. And our smile can have a profound effect on the people who see it. A smile is like the sun. It has the power to brighten up an entire day, sometimes an entire life.

Dale Carnegie (not Andrew) told us this story about a smile that was shown to him during the Great Depression in New York. Things seemed very bad for him, and he was depressed. He decided that it was the end, that he was going to take his own life by drowning in the river.

He came out of a building on the way to the river and almost immediately was hailed by a man who had no legs and sat on a skateboard. The man was obviously destitute and desperate. But he was smiling, and he said to Carnegie, "Mister, would you like to buy some pencils?"

Carnegie took out a dollar bill and handed it to the man and started to walk on.

The man rolled by him and yelled, "Hey, mister, you forgot your pencils."

Carnegie shook the man off, saying, "I don't want any pencils."

The fellow followed him for two blocks, insisting that either he take the pencils or take the money back, and what was astonishing to Carnegie was that the man was smiling the entire time. He finally took the pencils and realized that he no longer wanted to commit suicide. He later said, "I thought I had no reason to live until I saw a man who had no feet, yet had the power to smile."

A simple smile from another human being turned his life around. That's why we always suggest that you smile, particularly to strangers. The very act of smiling will make you feel better. And you never know how much difference it might make to them.

Try smiling in elevators. Here's an experiment. Walk into an elevator and instead of facing front, face the back and smile. It really throws people off guard. If you smile long enough, pretty soon they may even begin wondering what you've been up to that makes you so happy! More often than not, your smile will be returned, and not only will you have made someone else's day just a little bit better, but that person will have done the same thing for you.

Other Loving Techniques

There are other loving techniques that really don't need explanation, that are self-evident and that we should practice constantly. They are:

Maintain eye contact.
Hold hands.
Really listen.
When you're with someone, be totally there in the present moment.
Listen to positive love songs.
Always show tenderness and affection.
Be open and spontaneous.
Be responsive and interested.
Be well groomed, clean and smell pleasant.

Give flowers.
Share work, chores and playtime.
Give good morning and good night kisses.
Have a sense of humor.
Be cheerful.

The Ultimate Sacrifice

In this chapter we hope you've learned that love is available in abundance if we give ourselves away. Give your love to others and it will come back many times over.

One final demonstration of this great truth, a most eloquent one, is the story of Linda Birtish, who literally gave herself away. Linda was an outstanding teacher who felt that when she had time, she would like to create art and poetry. When she was twenty-eight, however, she began to get severe headaches. Her doctors discovered that she had an enormous brain tumor. They told her that her chances of surviving an operation were in the 2 percent range. Therefore, rather than operate immediately, they chose to wait six months.

She knew she had artistry in her. So during those six months she wrote and drew feverishly. All of her poetry, except one piece, was published in magazines. All of her art, except one piece, was shown and sold at some of the leading galleries.

At the end of six months, she had the operation. But the night before, she decided to give herself away—literally, physically. In case of her death, she wrote a will. In her will she donated all the parts of her body to those who needed them more than she would.

Unfortunately, Linda's operation was fatal. Subsequently her eyes went to an eye bank in Bethesda, Maryland, and from there to a recipient in South Carolina. A young man, age twenty-eight, went from darkness to sight. That young man was so profoundly grateful that he wrote to the eye bank thanking them for existing. It was only the second "thank you" that the eye bank had received after giving out in excess of thirty thousand eyes.

Furthermore, he said he wanted to thank the parents of the donor. They must indeed be magnificent folks to have a child who would give away her eyes. He was given the name of the Birtish family and went to see them on Staten Island. He flew in unannounced and rang the doorbell. After hearing his introduction, Mrs. Birtish hugged him to her bosom. She said, "Young man, if you've got nowhere to go, Dad and I would love for you to spend your weekend with us."

He stayed, and as he was looking around Linda's room, he saw that she'd read Plato. He'd read Plato in braille. She'd read Hegel. He'd read Hegel in braille.

The next morning Mrs. Birtish was looking at him and said, "You know, I've seen you somewhere before, but I don't know where." All of a sudden her "inner knowledge" triggered. She ran upstairs and pulled out the last picture Linda had ever drawn. It was a portrait of her ideal man.

Perhaps some readers can recall seeing this on the TV show "20/20." The picture was virtually identical to that young man.

Then her mother read the last poem Linda had written, on her deathbed. It read:

> Two hearts passing in the night
> falling in love
> never able to gain each other's sight.

The Joy of Marriage
and Family

*When you find your perfect other self, you will know it
in an instant.*

—KAHLIL GIBRAN

One of our favorite stories is about a man who dies, goes to
heaven, gets to the Pearly Gates and sees there are two doors.
On the left is one with a sign that reads, "For Non-Nagged
Husbands," and there's only one man in line.

On the right there's a door with a sign that says, "For
Nagged Husbands," and there are tens of thousands of men in
line.

The man asks the solitary fellow on the left, "What are you
doing standing over there?"

He replies, "My wife told me to stand here!"

Jokes about marriage are almost as old as the institution
itself. Whether one opts for marriage along with the stereo-

typed problems that go with it or not, we all have to deal with the issue.

In the last few years many seemingly successful people have dealt with it by opting for the single way of life, or some alternative lifestyle. For us, however, the finding of an ideal "other" to share our lives has proved to be the best and most natural way of fulfilling ourselves. We're not pedantically insisting that everyone should follow suit. We think that marriage has a lot to offer, and that it is something that has been, will be and should be pursued. (After all, if people didn't get married and have kids, where would we and you be today?)

We feel that, one way or another, the question of marriage and family has to be addressed by each of us, and each of us has to find his or her own satisfactory answers. Until we do, we will spend a disproportionate share of our energy on this question; we will be taking time and resources away from achieving our purpose and the majority of our goals. We need to resolve this issue in order to put our lives in balance.

The Search for Your Ideal "Other"

Early in life most of us begin searching for the perfect mate. It is the prelude to marriage and family. While for some lucky few the search can be short and easy, for most it is long and sometimes difficult. Many don't succeed in finding an ideal other until late in life. Some never do.

Part of the reason for the difficulty, and sometimes failure, to find the perfect mate can be our expectation. Until a few years ago, psychology books led us to believe that marital bliss occurred when two halves came together to form a whole. In other words, each of us was only half a person. It wasn't until we found that special "other" that we achieved wholeness. Thus many of us were wandering around looking for half a person.

Today, of course, very few espouse this half-and-half concept, because we realize it just isn't so.

The fact is that we are all whole, like whole circles. When we meet that special other, we combine and form a larger circle, one with even greater potential. Thus the search is for another whole person, someone with whom we can join, share and grow.

A Technique for Finding Your Perfect Partner

Every single person deserves to discover his or her ideal mate. Yet intentionally employing a strategy for finding that person is too rarely done.

Let's use the techniques described in earlier chapters. To begin, write down what you're looking for in a mate. Simply write out all the values, virtues, qualities, characteristics and personality traits you would like in your ideal other person. Attempt to be comprehensive and exhaustive.

Don't compromise. As a suggestion, you may want to do this in conjunction with another person who's also searching. Your combined efforts may produce more crystal-clear results. It doesn't make any difference if you live in a city or a small town. The act is the same and the results will happen.

The beauty of writing it all down is that it prevents making poor choices. It prevents the want-ad syndrome that ultimately states that you'll take this person or that one because he or she happens to be available.

One sixty-seven-year-old woman, who worked as a bookkeeper for a dentist in a rural area, heard Mark say, "You've got to admit that it might work, so why not do it? At least it's worth a try." She wrote down in great detail the qualities she'd look for in her ideal mate. Then, using the techniques outlined in earlier chapters, she visualized him and affirmed that he would appear.

Sure enough, within days a longtime supplier of dental products, whom she had never met other than by telephone, started sending little romantic notes on his invoices—a few sentences of innocent flirtation on each of three copies.

It made her feel good, so she responded in kind, hoping that her employer would never see these valentine scribblings. The love notes made her heart flutter. New life and spirit started flowing within her.

One day the dentist she worked for had an urgent need for a product, so she called her romantic pen pal to bring it in person. To her delight, she learned that he was seventy-two years young, available and wanted to marry her!

She said, "Yes!" They've now been cheerfully married for years. They still write love notes and remembrances to each other.

If you write it down, visualize it and affirm it, you can make it happen too.

Here is Glenna Salsbury's inspiring story:

Glenna's Goal Book

In 1977 I was a single mother with three young daughters, a house payment, a car payment and a need to rekindle some dreams.

One evening I attended a seminar and heard a man speak on the I $\times$ V = R Principle. (*Imagination mixed with Vividness becomes Reality.*) The speaker pointed out that the mind thinks in pictures, not in words. And as we vividly picture in our mind what we desire, it will become a reality.

This concept struck a chord of creativity in my heart. I knew the Biblical truth that the Lord gives us "the desires of our heart" (Psalms 37:4) and that "as a man thinketh in his

---

[1]Excerpted from *Chicken Soup for the Soul: 101 Stories to Open the Heart and Rekindle the Spirit*, by Jack Canfield and Mark Victor Han sen (Deerfield Beach, FL: Health Communications, 1993). Available at 1–800–433–2314.

heart, so is he" (Proverbs 23:7). I was determined to take my
written prayer list and turn it into pictures. I began cutting up
old magazines and gathering pictures that depicted the "desires of my heart." I arranged them in an expensive photo
album and waited expectantly.

I was very specific with my pictures. They included:

1. A good-looking man.
2. A woman in a wedding gown and a man in a tuxedo.
3. Bouquets of flowers. (I'm a romantic.)
4. Beautiful diamond jewelry. (I rationalized that God
   loved David and Solomon, and they were two of the richest men who ever lived.)
5. An island in the sparking blue Caribbean.
6. A lovely home.
7. New furniture.
8. A woman who had recently become vice-president of a
   large corporation. (I was working for a company that had
   no female officers. I wanted to be the first woman vice-
   president in that company.)

About eight weeks later, I was driving down a California freeway, minding my own business at 10:30 in the morning. Suddenly a gorgeous red-and-white Cadillac passed me. I looked
at the car because it was a beautiful car. And the driver looked
at me and smiled, and I smiled back because I always smile.
Now I was in deep trouble. Have you ever done that? I tried
to pretend that I hadn't looked. "Who me? I didn't look at
you!" He followed me for the next fifteen miles. Scared me to
death! I drove a few miles, he drove a few miles. I parked, he
parked and eventually I married him!

On the first day after our first date, Jim sent me a dozen
roses. Then I found out that he had a hobby. His hobby was
collecting diamonds. Big ones! And he was looking for some-

body to decorate. I volunteered! We dated for about two years, and every Monday morning I received a long-stemmed red rose and a love note from him.

About three months before we were getting married, Jim said to me, "I have found the perfect place to go on our honeymoon. We will go to St. John's Island down in the Caribbean." I laughingly said, "I never would have thought of that!"

I did not confess the truth about my picture book until Jim and I had been married for almost a year. It was then that we were moving into our gorgeous new home and furnishing it with the elegant furniture that I had pictured. (Jim turned out to be the West Coast wholesale distributor for one of the finest eastern furniture manufacturers.)

By the way, the wedding was in Laguna Beach, California, and included the gown and tuxedo as realities. Eight months after I created my dream book, I became the Vice-President of Human Resources in the company where I worked.

In some sense this sounds like a fairy tale, but it is absolutely true. Jim and I have made many "picture books" since we have been married. God has filled our lives with the demonstration of these powerful principles of faith at work.

Decide what it is that you want in every area of your life. Imagine it vividly. Then act on your desires by actually constructing your personal goal book. Convert your ideas into concrete realities through this simple exercise. There are no impossible dreams. And, remember, God has promised to give His children the desires of their heart.

Don't Go for a Particular Person

Please be careful to seek only the qualities of a person, not a particular person. Only emotionally immature people want movie stars such as Tom Selleck, Tom Cruise, Harrison Ford, Farrah Fawcett or Julia Roberts. There is little likelihood of marrying such a celebrity. Indeed, that celebrity may not have any of the qualities you would require in your perfect partner.

Instead, go for the values and virtues that you want the other person to have, such as sensitivity, loyalty, honesty, ambition and flexibility. You can certainly include physical attractiveness if that is important to you. For an exciting story about this kind of experience, we recommend that you read *Bridge Across Forever* by Richard Bach, author of *Jonathan Livingston Seagull*. In the book he found his ideal mate, and she matched the description he was looking for. But then he couldn't believe he was worthy of the love he had dreamily envisioned. Besides, he was stuck on the question, "Are you her?" "Are you her?" He almost missed his true love, Leslie Parrish Bach. He went through the tortures of the damned coming to terms with himself on this—but today he is happily married to her.

Mark's Story

Even if we do write out, visualize and affirm, how will we know when we have indeed met the perfect person for us? The answer is that we will know. Here is Mark's own personal experience to prove the point.

> *Love that lasts a lifetime is generated by our belief that it will last a lifetime.*

"For years before meeting my own perfect other, I had written down the following qualities that she must have: she should be an intellectual, and a voluptuary with self-disciplined tendencies toward hedonism (to each his own!).

"I was seriously dating another woman at the time I met my future wife. Patty was selling tickets outside a church to an upcoming Buckminster Fuller event that I was promoting throughout Southern California. I addressed the church service, which was packed and lacked air-conditioning, and I was a sweaty mess.

"Patty, seeing my problem, lovingly pulled my sweat-drenched shirt away from my perspiring body. Inwardly I thought that this was an unusual lady. Most women would think 'Yuck, sweat!' Not her. She wanted only to comfort me.

"After church we walked in a neighboring park. Suddenly a group of butterflies flew over to us, and it seemed that Patty had orchestrated their arrival. She had one light on the palm of her outstretched hand. She also had me hug a tree for the first time. And, apparently under her direction, a hummingbird fluttered like a helicopter directly in front of our faces. I thought that this must be an *akami* lady. *Akami* is a Hawaiian term for a person who really has it together and keeps it together.

"Then she offered to take me for a bicycle ride between Huntington Beach and Newport Beach, a lovely ride along the majestic Pacific Ocean. Before our ride, however, she took me to see her home. Homes are enormously important to me, as I travel so much. A home reflects the person who lives in it. I was particularly attracted to her kitchen ceiling, which was hand painted with clouds and birds flying overhead. We later redid this same theme on our living room wall.

"On the bicycle ride, Patty continued to open my heart in a magnificent yet subtle way. I was both startled and amazed. I had been to India in 1968 and had sat at the feet of a guru expecting what is called *shaktipat*—the experience of having one's heart opened. Yet I had never understood what I saw other students learning. Now, suddenly, I felt my heart opening. I received the knowledge. Patty opened my heart, which in thirty-one years had never felt anything like it.

"I felt it again when my babies, Elisabeth Day and, later, Melanie Dawn, were born. I gave each daughter their inaugural birthing bath in the labor room. The feeling was like a laser light of love that synchronized our two hearts.

"Believe me, when you find the perfect other for you, there will be no question and no doubt. You will know, and know that you know that you know."

Get Remarried Often

"While my wife and I were in a French bakery buying some fresh bread recently, the store clerk inquired, 'Are you together?'

"Patty responded, 'Yes, forever!'

"The clerk was amused, smiled, congratulated us and said, 'That's rare these days.'

"Once you've found the ideal mate, I urge you to reaffirm your vows on a regular, probably annual, basis. Some will scoff at this idea, but it's vitally important. It brings back to the conscious mind the reasons that you got married to begin with, and it also revives the romance and excitement of your early years. Plan to invite new friends and old. Videotape the proceedings. As children are added, make them part of the ceremony.

"My wife and I remarry on our anniversary. We send our re-wedding invitations to several hundred folks, write out our own vows and joyously get married in front of a minister.

"It is a touching and tearful event. When we get remarried we always look forward to an even more abundant and plentiful future."

> *Don't get married for "better or worse." Get married for "better and better."*

If you're thinking of writing your own vows or re-vows, we humbly offer these as suggestions. They are the first vows that Mark wrote:

I am getting married,
For more and more love,
For more and more romance, ecstasy and elation,
For better and better,
For more and more light, love and laughter,
For healthier and for healthier,
For richer and richer,
For more and more joy, bliss and happiness,
For more and more soul growth,
For the growth and support of Patty,
And for ninety-three years,
With options for renewal.

Here are Jack and Georgia's vows:

In the presence of God and these our family and friends, I declare my love for you. You are my beloved and my friend, and I choose you as my husband.

I vow, with you, to serve God's will to the best of my ability.

I vow, with you, to work to keep my consciousness as high and as pure as possible.

I vow to continually remind both of us of our true identity and our true purpose on earth.

I vow to be fearlessly honest with you, to seek the truth, share the truth, hear the truth and face the truth, to the best of my ability.

I vow, no matter what parts of yourself you reveal to me, to keep seeing the God in you, which is your highest potential and your true nature.

I affirm with you that our marriage is a marriage of soul, that through you and with you, I am marrying *God*.

As a gesture of my love and to seal these vows, I give you this ring.

I vow to stand with you and by you in holy union through whatever our journey may bring. To accept you, to love you and support you and to be thankful for all that we have and to share our life together in love forever.

You'll find in marriage whatever you expect to find. So why not program your marriage for ever-deepening love, romance, spiritual growth and fun?

We recommend and admonish you to be remarried annually in front of your priest, minister, rabbi or judge. People are living longer than ever before and having more stimuli and influences imprinted on them than ever before, so it's important to rededicate and recommit yourself to each other.

When you remarry, we suggest that you do as we do. Have a celebration and bring together lots of friends. Mark sends out a picture invitation that joyously represents his and Patty's annual marital evolution, like the addition of their daughters Elisabeth and Melanie. To commemorate these sacred, heartfelt events, they frame the invitations and hang them on a wall dedicated to "our loving memories." They have space for ninety-three framed portraits. The existing fourteen demonstrate their growth.

We recommend this technique to reinforce, remember and restate the loving and wonderful aspects of your own marriage. If you focus on love, you'll get more love. (If you plan on divorce, you'll realize that.)

We are the first generation in history that has studied in-depth marriage and relationships. The field of marriage counseling is less than fifty years old. Find out what model works and make your marriage extraordinary.

Children

Sooner or later, whether we've found the perfect mate or not, we've got to deal with the issue of children. Children can be our greatest joy, or they can draw off all our energy and shatter our lives.

Dr. Bill Cosby, as Dr. Cliff Huxtable on the enormously popular situation comedy, is one of our ideals of the perfect dad come to life. He demonstrated weekly how the perfect father should act. If you're a parent and you want instruction on raising your children, you could do far worse than to take your cue from *The Cosby Show*.

We personally enjoyed the show so much and believe so strongly in the redeeming values it espouses that we have videotaped and saved almost all of them so that we can review and learn from them in the presence of our evolving children.

> *"If a relationship is going to be a living art form of truth, it always has to be on the edge of chaos, looking at everything fresh—again and again."*
> —RAM DASS

The essence of raising children, of having children who daily bring us pleasure rather than pain, is in the art of communication. Children are not objects that we store on shelves in our homes. They are living, breathing, thinking, emoting human beings. If we maintain close communication with them, we will raise their self-esteem and our own. They will not draw off our energy, but instead will add to it.

The problem is that the average parents spend less than twelve-and-a-half minutes a day out of 168 available hours a week looking deeply into their kids' eyes and really communicating with them. What this means is that parents really don't take the time to learn about and be with their kids in a meaningful and communicative way. This is particularly the case when the children become teenagers. Parents of teenagers often respond, "My kids don't want to talk with me." It's mostly because the early pattern that was established was one of watching TV together but not communicating heart to heart.

Use your inner radar to find a family that communicates at depth and model them. Make your own a great example also.

It's certainly true that if we don't teach kids how to communicate when they're younger, it's harder when they are older. Regardless of their age, we owe it to our children to make the attempt. Even with teenagers, it's possible to reach them if we're open and honest and are willing to at least momentarily forgo the delusions of our own grandeur and see things from their perspective.

With young children, it's much easier. We can talk to these little ones and be articulate with them. When our children were babies and we went shopping with them, we would point out every vegetable and fruit and other items and introduce them to everyone in the store.

People say, "Why do you do that? She's just a baby."

We replied that at their own level children can ingest all that information. They can lock into it. Dr. Benjamine Bloom suggests that 70 percent of our IQ is gained by the time we are four years old. At this early age, children absorb all sorts of information, they can only learn more, and their retention level is perfect. Almost all children are born with a perfect mind and a perfect memory. The truth is that we don't even begin to suspect what they're taking in. Thus the more stimuli, the more positive the attitude, the more information about the world that we can communicate to them, the better it will be for them and ultimately for us in our relationship with them. Dr. Buckminster Fuller said, "A parent's goal is to give [children] progressively less misinformation than we got."

Self-Esteem in Kids

Depending on how they were raised, kids have higher or lower levels of self-esteem. Low self-esteem in a child is a symptom of a problem that requires our immediate and close attention.

A research study done at the University of Iowa showed

that the average two-year-old receives 432 negatively oriented statements a day to 32 positive ones. That's a 14-to-1 ratio. No wonder so many kids feel beaten down and have low self-esteem today. National statistics indicate only 35 percent of all youth in America have high self-esteem. That's one out of three!

Here is a list of negative rules and negative messages commonly heard in American families that Dr. Charles Whitfield compiled for his book *Healing the Child Within:*

Negative Rules	**Negative Messages**
Don't express your feelings	Shame on you
Don't get angry	You're not good enough
Don't get upset	I wish I'd never had you
Don't cry	Your needs are not all right with me
Do as I say, not as I do	Hurry up and grow up
Be good, "nice," perfect	Be dependent
Avoid conflict (or avoid dealing with conflict)	Be a man
Don't think or talk; just follow directions	Big boys don't cry
Do well in school	Act like a nice girl (or a lady)
Don't ask questions	You don't feel that way
Don't betray the family	Don't be like that
Don't discuss the family with outsiders; keep the family secret	You're so stupid (or bad, etc.)
Be seen and not heard	You caused it
No back talk	You owe it to us
Don't contradict me	Of course we love you!
Always look good	I'm sacrificing myself for you
I'm always right, you're always wrong	How can you do this to me?
Always be in control	We won't love you if you . . .
Focus on the alcoholic's drinking (or troubled person's behavior)	You're driving me crazy!

Drinking (or other troubled behavior) is not the cause of our problems

Always maintain the status quo

Everyone in the family must be an enabler

You'll never accomplish anything

It didn't really hurt

You're so selfish

You'll be the death of me yet

That's not true

I promise (though breaks it)

You make me sick!

We wanted a boy/girl

Determining self-esteem problems isn't difficult. If you have a youngster at or near the teenage years, we're sure you've had at least one experience with 900 numbers. These are numbers that can be called from any phone to receive a recorded message. There's a flat fee for the call, usually anywhere from fifty cents to two dollars per minute.

Lots of kids have been calling these numbers, and psychologists say that the reason is low self-esteem. The kids feel badly about themselves, so they're calling these numbers just to listen to somebody talk who feels better than they do. Some kids have spent hundreds of dollars of their parents' phone-bill money on these calls.

When we encounter such low self-esteem, it's time for us as parents to make an active effort toward positive change. If we don't act at the outset, we may be faced with runaways, drugs, pregnancies—a host of problems that will unbalance our lives for years.

The easiest way to develop strong self-esteem in our children is to embody it ourselves. The kids then have a model to follow and can mold themselves accordingly. It's for this reason we have major seminars annually that involve parents and their teenagers. Teenagers learn that their parents are real and have needs and feelings, and are human.

If you have any doubt as to the value of this process, remember the story told by Hans Christian Andersen, the Danish fable writer. He once wrote of a king who had a five-year-old son with a crooked back (scoliosis). To correct the problem, the king simply had a statue made of his young son, identical in every likeness except one: the statue showed his son with a straight back and perfect posture.

The king placed this statue in the boy's play area and gently remarked how healthy, happy and royal the boy looked. He mentioned that if he stood tall as a king, he would have the wisdom and vision to rule his kingdom. As the boy grew, his back straightened until one day he was just as straight and tall as the statue. It was easy for him, since he had a perfect model to follow. We all model the mental equivalents we have in our mind's eye.

Tell Them They're Terrific

Another method of building self-esteem in kids, and this applies when they're younger than teenagers, is to tell them that they're terrific. If we tell them straight out, of course, they'll think it's a con job and they won't listen. So the way to really do it is to tell someone else about them, but within their hearing.

Mark's mother was a master at letting him eavesdrop on what she was saying. She knew he wouldn't listen to whatever she said directly to him. Mark remembers that when she talked to her friends—we think she and the neighbors were in cahoots—she would say, "I have the best boys on the block." Mark says, "This made us determined to grow up to become the best boys on the block, which we did. All my brothers (I have no sisters) have become outstanding family men, businesspeople and contributors to society. It worked."

Facing Up to Marriage and Family

Each of us must deal with and resolve the issue of finding a perfect spouse and of rearing a family. We encourage everyone to go face-to-face with it. If you are looking for your perfect mate, use the methods of goal writing, visualizing and affirmation to find him or her. If you've found each other and have decided to raise a family, spend the time communicating with your children, giving them self-esteem, guiding them as teenagers and young adults.

If you actively work at it, the reward will be a joyous life. There is little that will bolster our own self-esteem more, and that will keep our lives more in balance, than having an ideal mate and a happy family.

When our lives are complete, we have good memories and loved ones. It's comforting to be surrounded by loved ones who love you still, and want to hold your hand, as taught in the hospice movement, when you exit your life with dignity, class, joy and serenity.

Achieving Total Prosperity

"Earn as much as you can,
Save as much as you can,
Invest as much as you can,
Give as much as you can."
—REVEREND JOHN WELLESLY

You can achieve total prosperity!

You can have all that you want financially and more.

You can have joy and success and money in your future—much more than you've had in your past.

All it takes to achieve this is the proper state of mind. Prosperity is created by a state of mind.

The principle is simple: get turned on about prosperity and stay turned on. Write down your prosperity goals, visualize them, affirm your prosperity regularly, take appropriate actions, and you will achieve them!

Prosperity Creates Freedom

It is better to have more money than less. It is better to accumulate it faster than slower. Money increases life's options. It creates new kinds of freedom and ends the slavery of poverty.

We don't think anyone would disagree. Now, the questions we all ask are "How do we get it?" "Where does prosperity start?" "How do we find the source?" If we want to be prosperous, we know we have to begin somewhere, but where?

The answer is simple. Prosperity starts with an idea. Become convinced that it's available, persuade yourself to obtain it, and accept it as it arrives. Then, if you are positive about it, you breathe life and form into it.

The second prerequisite is that the idea must be positive. What's a positive idea?

Back in 1971, when Mark was launching his first business, he was in Boulder, Colorado, with his friend Moe Siegel. They were both full of wonderful buoyant energy. They'd go up and watch the sunset in what's called the "flatirons" of Boulder.

Moe would always be picking seeds and herbs, and he was saying, "Someday I'll have a tea company to rival Lipton." Everyone always said, "Yeah, sure, sure."

Well, he started by selling his little teas to health food stores. Then he began expanding, and before long he was selling them to every chain in America. Today we all know his brand as Celestial Seasonings tea, one of the biggest employers in Colorado.

Did Moe start out with money? Did he start out with a big factory or warehouse? Did he have a giant corporation behind him? Was he negative?

The answer to all four questions is *No*. He started on the road to prosperity simply with an idea and the courage to believe in it.

You start with the idea, nurture it, cherish it like a helpless little baby. It will grow. You'll have other ideas flash into your mind that will tell you how you can do it. Then you do it!

The Idea Book

Ira Hayes, one of our country's foremost authorities on positive thinking, known as the Ambassador of Enthusiasm, suggests that everything starts with an idea: the safety pin, the Polaroid camera, sunglasses, Band-Aids, automatic dishwashers, ballpoint pens, even the board game Monopoly. He suggests that the fruitful applications of ideas are endless.

Ira goes on to suggest that we should have an "Idea of the Week Book." For his own "Idea of the Week Book," he annually writes numbers 1 through 52 for each year, on consecutive pages in a binder. As a result, he generates 52 ideas a year. He has successfully programmed his mind to look for one creative, success-promoting idea for every week of the year, every year for the past thirty years. It made him the most famous person in NCR and a top speaker, who, once heard, is unforgettable.

We think it's a great idea. We think we should all carry idea books around with us. After all, ideas can be elusive things. One minute they dominate our minds, the next they're gone. The rule seems to be, "Write them down while you think of them."

Entrepreneurship

If what we've said so far sounds like starting your own business, you're on the right track. Look at it this way. If you're an entrepreneur, you've got a positive idea that you're forming into reality. If you're a salaried employee, you're working for someone else, and that other person is the guy who has the positive idea and is reaping the rewards. Why not be the one with the idea yourself?

Historically, for someone to be really prosperous, that person has had to be an entrepreneur. That means a risk taker who runs his or her own free-enterprise business, whether it is a little mom-and-pop shop, a country club joint venture or whatever.

Today the new word is "intra-preneurship." That's someone who takes an idea to an existing company. The company manufactures it, sells it, distributes it and gives the idea person a piece of the action. It means getting paid for being the creative genius behind it all.

A quick example of intra-preneurship is Arthur Fry of the 3M Company. Fry kept losing his paperwork. He was disorganized and couldn't keep track of notes he had written to himself. He discovered that his own company, 3M, had invented a glue that didn't stick well. It would hold a piece of paper to something, but you could quickly peel it off. Fry put his needs and that glue together and came up with an idea. They tested it for one year at 3M before they put it on the market. It's called a Post-it.® For coming up with that idea and giving it to 3M, Fry got 1 percent of the action for life. Annually 3M sells over $100 million worth of Post-its. Fry receives $1 million a year for that one idea. You can do the same or better.

In the past, if we had an idea, we had to go into development and production and distribution and advertising and so forth. Today we can let a company take care of it. The money goes to the idea.

All of us have ideas! We're idea mines. An estimate is that the average person has a hundred ideas a day, plus or minus a few. What we need to do is write them all down. Keep them in a file or in your computer. Prioritize them, focus on the best one, harvest it and then make a decision to run with it. Later, harvest the rest systematically and sequentially. Act on the easiest and most profitable idea(s) first. The cash flow will permit you to act on your other ideas.

Ideas Are Everywhere

A hair stylist recently felt that she and her baby were unsafe when they were in an automobile. She felt that if other drivers knew about the baby, they would feel the same as she did and take extra precautions. So she came up with a little sticker to alert them. It just said, "Baby on Board." She put it in her rear window, and to her amazement, it worked! This lady told herself that if it worked for her, it would work for others, so she went to J. C. Penney and sold the idea to them. She has been making a fortune each month on the royalties.

One of Mark's clients, who is one of the owners of Citizens Against Crime, was concerned because people are so vulnerable when their cars break down on the highway. At that time, someone with criminal intent can take advantage of them. So he made a little sign to keep in your glove compartment for emergencies. It says, "Call Police." They sell it for six dollars apiece. He's also rolling in his royalties.

As we said, ideas are everywhere. Sometimes they'll pop out of what we're doing. Sometimes they are a matter of necessity. Forty years ago, a mother down in La Jolla, California, went to her thirty-year-old son, who was a well-known medical researcher. She said, "Jonas, your brother is dying of polio. Why don't you find a cure for it?"

He looked at her and said something like, "Mom, I never took it as my own commitment or responsibility. But I love my brother more than myself, so I'll do it." He proceeded to work twenty-four hours a day, seven days a week until he came up with the Salk vaccine.

The 12 Steps to Prosperity

We've talked about what prosperity is and how it comes from positive ideas. Now we'd like to give you twelve steps to achieve it.

STEP 1

Don't Focus on the Problem

If all you are looking for is the problem, then all you'll find is the problem. If you're faced with poverty and concentrate on that poverty, then what you'll get is more poverty.

Poverty means that you can't meet your family's needs. It means that when the tires on your car are bald, you can't get new ones. It means medical assistance is not affordable to you. Your child's education is out of reach financially. It means that you can't take a vacation and you can't travel to see your family on holidays.

In *Think and Grow Rich*, Napoleon Hill says, "When riches come, they come in such abundance that you begin wondering where they've been hiding during all the lean years!"

STEP 2

Think Prosperous Thoughts

Remember, before you achieve it, prosperity is an *attitude.* We had an earthquake not long ago in California, where we live. Little Johnny, who's five years old, comes running in after the earthquake, and his mother says, "Johnny, where were you?"

He replies, "Honest, Mom, I didn't do it!"

We like little Johnny stories because they show that his attitude was set up to be negative. He was set up for being blamed no matter what happened, even an earthquake. Therefore, he created the situation he wanted to avoid.

On the other hand, the right attitude can absolutely create prosperity. We offer the example of Dr. Armand Hammer. Back in the early part of this century, when he was twenty-one years old and in medical school, disaster hit his family. His father, Dr. Julius Hammer, owned a pharmaceutical chain that was having difficulties. One day his father was accused of performing an abortion in which a girl died. He was convicted and sent to jail.

Suddenly Armand was faced with taking over the pharmaceutical company. He was only two years from graduation; now school seemed impossible, but Armand didn't focus on the problem. Instead, he looked around to see what avenues to prosperity were open.

It was the start of Prohibition. The classic story of the period was that a drunk was brought into court to see a judge. The judge said, "You're here for drinking."

To which the drunk replied, "I'm ready if you are!"

Booze was what people wanted, and Hammer realized that tincture of ginger was what was needed to make bootleg gin. He went out and cornered the world market on tincture of ginger, making a two-million-dollar fortune on one idea.

Immediately he had the finances and hired Louis Nizer, the premier attorney of the period, to argue his father's case. He soon had his father out of jail. Armand remained responsible for the pharmacies. So he went home at night after shutting down the stores and studied from eight in the evening until one in the morning. He couldn't attend classes, so he hired another student to take notes for him. At the end of the year, he took all the tests and graduated number one in his medical class at Columbia University! Then he sold the pharmacies to the employees and made his first million.

> *Go for the luxuries and the necessities will take care of themselves.*

Young Dr. Hammer wanted to go into practice, but adversity struck again. It would be six months before he could practice medicine at Bellevue Hospital. What should he do with the time? Dr. Hammer's father, a Russian and a socialist, told him he'd heard that people were dying of bubonic plague in Russia. So Dr. Hammer put together a little medical wagon and by boat and train got to Russia.

When he arrived he found that the people weren't dying of bubonic plague; instead, they were starving to death. Hammer used his million dollars to buy wheat and ship it to Russia. This earned him Lenin's personal attention. When they met, Lenin told Hammer that Russia needed tractors for growing crops, and commerce to bring in more foodstuffs. Lenin said, "I need a businessman, not a doctor."

Hammer went home and called on Henry Ford. He told Ford he wanted tractors for the Russians. Ford called him a pinko, a Soviet Bolshevik sympathizer, and told him to get out.

> *Spectacular success is preceded by spectacular, although invisible, mental preparation.*

Hammer did his homework. He realized that although Ford was selling cars like hotcakes, he was having trouble selling the tractors he had just invented. American farmers didn't understand the need for such expensive horses just yet. He went back and said, "Mr. Ford, I know you don't like Communists. I'm a free enterpriser myself. So I'll make you a business deal. For every two tractors you sell me, I'll buy one car from you."

Ford agreed. Hammer got his tractors, resold the cars for a profit and shipped the tractors to Russia. The Russians used them to start harvesting food to feed their population. In return, Hammer earned the right to thirty-eight major trade concessions, each of which was worth a fortune. He was on his way to becoming a billionaire.

Again adversity struck. Stalin took over, cancelled all the concessions and gave Hammer twenty-four hours to get out of Russia. Dr. Hammer made one last request before leaving.

Could he take with him the old czarist artwork he had collected from around Russia? Stalin and the Communists hated the works, so his request was granted.

During the height of our Depression, Hammer arrived in New York with the artwork. He took it to the Metropolitan Museum of Art, but they couldn't afford to buy the collection, so he asked them if he could organize a show. The admission would be fifty cents and he and the Met would split fifty-fifty. Armand's brother Victor said, "It's the Depression. Who can afford to attend an art show?" Dr. Hammer said, "No matter how hard the economy is, people always have a little money, especially for entertainment."

Well, the show was an amazing success. *Millions* came to see it, and in just a few weeks, Hammer, who had been financially ruined by Stalin, was a millionaire again! In good times and bad times, ideas make millionaires. Affirm every night for a month, "I have a million-dollar idea that I can make come true for me now." That positive self-suggestion will stimulate your subconscious into right action, right now.

A Prosperous Attitude Always Wins

What's so instructive about Dr. Armand Hammer's story, and why we've devoted so much space to it, is that the man personifies a prosperous attitude. Nothing could happen to him that could keep him from being prosperous. His prosperity didn't come from, or depend on, other people, world events or even luck. His prosperity came entirely from within. It came from his attitude. He simply refused to accept defeat, or even discouragement.

Countless times Hammer had been laid low by circumstance. Others would have focused on their problems. Hammer focused on the solution. He *knew* he would be prosperous again. It was simply a matter of putting together the right ideas to make it happen. Because Hammer continually had prosperous thoughts, he had a prosperous life. He lived until he was ninety-three years old and was a medical doctor, business-man, human treasure, art collector, philanthropist and world server. We suggest you read his autobiography and his picto-rial autobiography.

```
┌─────────────────────────────────────┐
│              STEP 3                  │
└─────────────────────────────────────┘
```

Don't Believe in Hard Times

You've heard the old joke about hard times. When your friends are unemployed, it's a recession. When you are unemployed, it's a depression. Well, don't you believe it.

People get stuck in their beliefs about the economy. If we worry that there's inflation or deflation, our attitude will cause us to have difficulty because of recession or inflation.

The farmers in the Midwest are having a particularly hard time as we write this. In fact, one farmer I talked with said, "About the only way to make a deposit on a John Deere tractor today is to hire a pigeon!"

That's not a bad line, but it's a terrible *attitude*. No matter how tough things get, you just can't let them get to *you*. You've got to program yourself to keep expecting—and generating—*boom* times. If you keep a boom-times attitude, *you'll* soon be booming. Our minds and our imaginations can help us to ride out, to rise above—and even prosper in—times of both reces-sion and inflation.

In business, the standard procedure is to tighten the belt during lean periods in the economy. Not so in highly success-ful companies. It was during a recession that Bill Marriott expanded his hotel chain while others were pulling back. He virtually doubled the size of his company during that period. His philosophy was that while everyone else was laying off, he would hire—at lower salaries—superior people who would be grateful to receive work.

During a recession, Delta Airlines doubled the number of airplanes they owned. They told their employees, "We're going to keep all of you working." The employees were so thankful they helped Delta pay for the planes!

So hard times are nothing more than a state of mind. Change your state of mind and you can change the quality of your life, no matter what happens to the economy.

```
┌─────────────────────────────────────┐
│                                      │
│            STEP  4                   │
│                                      │
└─────────────────────────────────────┘
```

Allow Prosperity to Find You

So many of us do the very same thing over and over just to earn a buck and never see the millions out there waiting for us. If we're going to be prosperous, it's important not to be locked into a single way of thinking.

Getting locked in, for us, might mean that we think of ourselves as being just speakers and writers. But suppose an opportunity for making money suddenly appears in, say, leisure activities. If we're locked into who we think we are, we lock it out; we snub the idea because it's not in our arena. Suggestion: start thinking of your arena as becoming and staying prosperous. Anything and everything that furthers your progress toward that goal is what you should be concerned with.

> *We're each either a thermometer or a thermostat. We either register someone else's temperature or our own.*

Be a thermostat, controlling your life, your emotions and feelings and how you experience conditions.

If we're open to prosperity, then the opportunities will descend on us and we'll have trouble just raking it in. It's like the old adage "The rich get richer . . ." All we have to do is think rich.

STEP 5

My Prosperity Makes Everyone Better Off

Some people are afraid to be prosperous because they think they're taking their prosperity out of someone else's mouth. They seem to think that there's just so much to go around. If I take more, someone else has to take less. When computers came into popularity everyone feared for their jobs; in reality, computers created more jobs, not less, and more sophisticated, thoughtful work. This is true because the universe is fundamentally abundant, and technology can share haveness universally and still be ecologically considerate.

This is not the kind of thinking that most of us were brought up on as kids. We thought that if you had something good, then something bad would happen to make you pay for it. We thought there was a compensating balance to the universe. If we had only a dime to spend and everyone wanted an ice cream cone, only one person could have it.

Buckminster Fuller taught us that this was foolishness. He demonstrated that there's enough prosperity, enough money in the universe right now for each of the five billion people who are alive to become millionaires—with ample resources left over for their children yet to be born.

It's no longer how big the piece of pie is, it's how big you make the pie. If the pie in your mind is small, all you need to do is expand your mind to create a bigger pie.

We can remember back when TV first came out. The movie-makers started crying the blues. As if TV would be so cheap that no one would go to the movies anymore. Making movies would be a dying art. Did that happen? Hardly. The movie-makers started selling their product to TV. The theater owners started showing better quality movies. Multiple movie theaters sprung up. *The pie got bigger.* Everyone became more pros-perous.

Just a few years ago, VCRs made their big impact on the scene, and again moviemakers were crying. Who would go to theaters or watch network TV anymore? Everyone would be watching movies on their VCRs.

Did it happen? Again, no. Moviemakers began selling to VCR owners through video shops. At the beginning of 1986, the VCR movie market became bigger than the theatrical mar-ket! But millions of people are still lining up at theaters. The pie got bigger again. There was more for everyone. The more prosperous each person in the field became, the bigger the field became, the more people were employed and the more money everyone made.

The principle behind all this is that a good deal is a good deal for everyone. If it's only a good deal for you, it's not a good deal. It has to be win/win.

STEP 6

Get Past "Stuckedness"

"Stuckedness" happens to all of us occasionally. It's when we have a problem and we get stuck on it. We try to move beyond the problem, but we can't. And as we've seen, if we don't get beyond the level of a problem, all we get is more problem.

Joggers wake up occasionally and just can't put on their

running shoes. Marathon runners "hit the wall" and just can't go on. Writers get "writer's block." Salespeople just can't make another "cold call." Investors get "down on the market." It happens to all of us at one time or another.

What's important is not to stay with it, not to let it get a grip on you. For a jogger, the answer is to put on those jogging shoes and get out there anyway. Joggers who force themselves to run, even when they don't want to, report that they feel amazingly better when the process is over.

Marathon runners do it with heart. Their body says no, but their heart says yes. When they've broken through the physical wall, their mental energy soars. Writers get started again just by writing. They sit down and write something easy. When they've finished, they feel they've earned the right to continue communicating. The block is broken.

The ABC of decisions is always be deciding.

Salespeople just start calling again, unbearable as it may seem. When the voice on the other end of the line starts responding, their confidence and self-esteem grow to the point where they can make calls for hours.

Investors get their feet wet in the market again. As soon as they have money back at risk, they feel a little bit better. And when they make a few dollars, they start feeling terrific again and can move on.

Regardless of where you may be stuck, the answer is the same, *Take action!* Do the very thing you don't want to do. It's like "chlorine lock" in a swimming pool. The impurities in water lock the chlorine up so it can't work. The cure? Add more chlorine.

When you get to "stuckedness," close your eyes and patiently allow your "inner knower" to come up with the answer. Believe and be confident, and you will either immediately or ultimately have the answer.

STEP 7

Don't Quit, No Matter What

As we learned from the tortoise and the hare, persistence pays off. It may take a little while for prosperity to hit, but it will arrive.

Joel Weldon, a motivational speaker from Phoenix, taught us this with a little story about a Chinese bamboo farmer who planted bamboo on his farm and then waited. The first year nothing came up. The second year there was still nothing to be seen. Same for the third year, and the fourth. By the fifth year there were a million miles of root systems underneath the ground, and when the bamboo finally broke through the earth, it grew more than a foot a day. In just six weeks, it was more than sixty feet tall. So the farmer harvested the bamboo and became wealthy.

As the old Confucian adage says, everything comes to he who waits. We would add a little extra: Just be sure you've planted the seeds. The trouble is—to change the metaphor—that too many people wait for their ships to come in, but they are waiting at the bus depot!

STEP 8

Promise a Lot—and Deliver Even More

If we're going to become prosperous, we're going to need the aid of others. We'll need them to buy our products, our services, ourselves. But in the real world, there will be others also endeavoring in the same niche. How do we win in such a situation? How do we do better, make more, achieve greater results than the competition? The answer is simple: we promise a lot, and deliver *more*.

It's the little things that make the difference. In a good motel, they deliver a clean room with a bed. In a great motel, they deliver crisp sheets, a piece of candy on the pillow at night and coffee and a paper in the morning.

There are people selling everything imaginable to everyone possible out there in the world. Those who make the sales are the ones who remember the names of clients' spouses and children, who offer a little fringe benefit, a little something extra that others don't.

You have to *deliver* to win. You have to deliver *more* to become prosperous.

STEP 9

Get in the Right Career

When you meet someone for the first time, chances are the first question they are likely to ask is "What do you do for a living?" The reason is that work is the biggest block of time we allocate to anything. It's also tied in with our self-esteem. People believe that we *are* what we do. As soon as they can identify what we do, they feel as though they have a handle on us, that they know us.

We feel sorry for the vast majority of people who live lives of quiet desperation in unfulfilling occupations, who have neglected planning for joy in their careers. If we really are what we do, then we had better put a lot more thought into it than most of us do.

We sincerely hope that *you're* doing what you want to do

with your whole head, heart, mind and body. If not, we suggest you probe yourself mentally and ask, "Where is it that I'd like to make my contribution?" If you have trouble answering that question, look to where you do your best work. Look for what only you do so well. Were you doing it before you began to work for a living? Did you do it for a living once and then quit? Have you been so involved in making a living that you've *never* really tried it? If so, then the probability is high that there's where you ought to be spending your time professionally. Decide to do it. Write it, visualize it, affirm it. And you'll soon be doing it!

We both enjoy speaking. We enjoy it so much we'd do it even if it were for free! (Don't let any of the people who hire us hear that!) The point is that speaking is our natural best career. It's what we do so well.

Do you think it's too late for you? No way. It's never too late to forge a rewarding career. Mark's father retired at the age of fifty-three from owning a bakery business. But he couldn't stay retired. He felt that he had to be doing what he did so well. So he began delivering "meals on wheels" to older people. He said, "Somebody's got to feed those old fogies!"

He had a physical problem with his eyes, his depth perception, so they took his driver's license away from him. Then he began delivering those "meals on wheels" by bicycle! He was old, but not too old to have rewarding work. We're never too old, as long as we're alive. We'll live a lot longer if we love the work we do.

STEP 10

The Five Rules for Making Money

Apply these five rules and it's impossible to go wrong!

1. *Earn the money.* Most people think this is the hardest.

It's actually the easiest. On page 116 of this chapter, we discussed several ways, including "intra-preneurship" and other techniques. Here is another:

Use leverage. People frequently think of leverage only in terms of real estate. That's unfortunate, because leverage has other uses. Here are four items that we can leverage:

A. *Money.* The rule here is to use OPM—other people's money. There are countless books on the market, including Robert Allen's *Nothing Down,* that tell us how to do this.

B. *Ideas.* Use ideas to leverage yourself up. If you have good ideas, they will attract money. The ideas themselves will accomplish great things for you. Reread the first few pages of this chapter to be sure you're crystal-clear on this.

C. *Time.* In roughly the last hundred years, humanity has moved from the horse and buggy to the Mach III jet plane. And the rate at which speed is increasing has itself increased. If we can learn to do the same thing with our own personal time, we can multiply our productivity and our income. If you decrease the time you take to accomplish some wealth-building task, for example, then you will have time left over for building more wealth.

D. *People.* We personally think that the most dramatically successful idea for the rest of this century for leveraging people is MLM (multi-level-marketing, sometimes referred to as networking marketing). Just imagine if you had a hundred people working for you and you were making only 5 percent of their $100,000 income, that's $50,000 a year. That's leveraging people. Our friend, Mark Yarnell, a Nu-Skin distributor in Reno, Nevada, has 50,000 people in his downline and earns 1.5 million dollars.

Add this technique to the others we've already discussed, and making the money will indeed become the easiest part.

2. *Save the money.* If you want to become rich, saving is the key. John Savage, a thoughtful and original financial planner, says, "People who invest before they save are ignorant idiots."

If you earned $40,000 a year for your entire worklife of fifty years, you would have earned two million dollars. If you save 10 percent, that's $200,000. Wisely invested in a prudent mutual fund, that can make you rich and financially free.

You may be asking, "How can I get rich just by saving? Don't I need to invest in the stock market to get rich?" What many of the richest people in this country have discovered is the law of compounding interest. Banks use it when they make loans. We can use it when we save.

The way it works is simple. If we deposit $10 and earn 5 percent interest, at the end of the term we have $10.50. If we keep that $10 on deposit, we now earn interest not only on the original $10 but on the 50¢ as well. Thus, at the end of the next term our money has grown to $11.03. Just by saving our money in a compound-interest-bearing account, our money grows at an accelerating rate.

The real question when saving, therefore, is not whether or not our money will grow, but how fast it will grow. To help answer this, we have the "Rule of 72," a shorthand method of determining how quickly our money will double at any given interest rate.

To use it, just divide the interest you're receiving on your money into the number 72. The result is the time it takes to double that money. For example, if the interest rate received is 10 percent, just divide 10 into 72 and you'll discover it will take 7.2 years to double that money. Here's a quick breakdown of the rule for various interest rates:

Interest Rate	Time to Double Money
0	Forever!
5	14.4 years
10	7.2 years
15	4.8 years
20	3.6 years

3. *Increase net worth.* There are seven ways to increase our net worth. They are:

A. *Put money in the bank, obviously.*
B. Buy life insurance.
C. Invest in art, antiques and collectibles.
D. Buy stocks, bonds and mutual funds.
E. Invest in gold, silver and diamonds.
F. Own your own business.
G. Purchase and hold real estate.

Don't try to accomplish all of these at once. Together they may seem an enormous burden. But spread out over a lifetime, they are all easily achievable.

4. *Tithe.* Some people are going to wonder why we have put tithing under rules for making money. The reason is that tithing is a universal spiritual principle. If we give back 10 percent of our total income to God through our church, temple, synagogue, mosque or our favorite charity or nonprofit organization, in return we will receive greater abundance.

Tithing teaches us, "Give and you shall receive." God gives us 100 percent of what we need to facilitate His work and underwrite miracles in our lives. He requests that only 10 percent of that be given back.

Mark wrote *The Miracle of Tithing*[1] to answer the myriad of questions laypeople ask about this virtually unknown principle. The belief is that if 100 percent of humanity tithed 10 percent, the spiritual world would allow the physical world to be totally and successfully at peace.

5. *Be a philanthropist.* Tom Wolfe says, "Others have paved the roads that we are traveling and dug the wells from which we are drinking. We owe those who follow us to provide new roads and new wells for them." Each of us is a member of society. After we have achieved an acceptable standard of living, we have a "civic rent" to pay. We owe back to the systems that have provided so generously for us. When we are asked to volunteer time, thought, money, talent, leadership or energy to our community, church or association, we should do so, when it lies within our abilities.

People who have their own personal lives organized are banding together to do something and take action for others on a vast and attention-grabbing scale. Performers Michael Jackson and Lionel Ritchie got together and said, "We've got to do something for Ethiopian relief." They conceived the "We Are the World" song.

Through this historic song, teenagers saw a new business model for cooperation rather than competition. Forty-three major celebrities put their egos aside and got together *without* pay to contribute their vocal talents to one of the most heart-filled, emotionally stimulating songs and videos of all time. It was philanthropy at its best. It made everyone feel good to participate. More than $40 million was raised.

Its success led to other, similar philanthropic activi-

---

[1]*The Miracle of Tithing*, by Mark Victor Hansen, is available for $4.00 from M.V. Hansen & Associates, Inc. PO Box 7665, Newport Beach, Calif 92627. 1-800-433-2314.

ties, such as the Live Aid Concert, to which promoters Bob Geldorf and Bill Graham and dozens of renowned performers donated their efforts. More than 1 billion people tuned in as concerts were held simultaneously in London and Philadelphia.

Ken Kragen stretched "Hands Across America" with millions of us participating. We all paid to help the needy in America. Mark's family and staff held hands on a picturesque riverbed in Yorba Linda, California. Jack's family and staff were on San Vicente Boulevard in Brentwood, California. There were no celebrities in either location, just people volunteering to be in the longest, most philanthropic human chain in history.

The philanthropy you participate in will mark the kind of person you are. Others will note it, and it will come back to you in multiple ways.

But what can I do personally? We're sure this is a question that many of you are asking.

Consider the case of a super human being—Del Smith, founder and chairman of the board of Evergreen Airlines, the largest private airline in America. Mark was visiting with Del in McMinnville, Oregon, and they were discussing philanthropy. Instead, the subject of kids and free enterprise came up. Del is strongly for free enterprise at even an early age. To understand why, you have to understand Del.

He was orphaned at the age of seven, and Grandma Smith took him into her house. She told him, "We believe in work and opportunity here." She gave him a copy of *Think and Grow Rich* by Napoleon Hill.

Del was inspired. At the tender age of seven years old, he courageously went down to the bank and borrowed $2.50. He proceeded across the street to another bank and borrowed $2.50 more. With it he bought a lawn mower.

Del cut lawns for 15¢ a lawn. He said, "Some looked as big as a golf course." By 1941 he was eleven years old and had saved $100. On his own initiative, he proceeded to buy a $1,200 house for Grandma Smith with a $100 down payment.

When he went to college, she allowed him to borrow money out of the equity in the house to complete his education. Upon graduation he entered the Air Force, only to discover he was color-blind. When they wouldn't let him fly, he told himself, *"That's okay, I'm an entrepreneur. When I get out, I'll earn enough money and buy my own helicopter."* Del had been in college when Sikorsky invented the helicopter, and he felt sure it was destined to become the workhorse of aviation.

Well, when he mustered out at age twenty-five, he did buy his first one, and Del Smith is now running a worldwide company with twenty-six operating divisions.

One day in his office, between seminars for his company, Del said to Mark, "There's one thing kids can't do anymore." Mark asked, "What's that?"

"They can no longer borrow money from a bank."

Mark said, "Let's start a kids' bank." He then left for a one-hour tour of the helicopter plant. When he returned, Del's senior VP, Donna Nelson, told him, "Good news. Del has just started the 'Mark Victor Hansen Free Enterprise Bank' and given it $25,000 as a nonprofit operation." What a marvelous philanthropic act!

When the bank commissioners later closed the bank down, because it was illegal for kids to sign a contract, Del called in his lawyers and said, "Figure out a way to make the bank work." They did. They no longer lend children money, they grant it. They changed the name to the Mark Victor Hansen Children's Free Enterprise Fund, Inc.

The fund grants money to kids, but they expect them to pay it back with interest so that future generations can borrow it again. Hundreds of kids across the nation have received money for various projects and 100 percent have repaid. They are learning valuable lessons in free enterprise.

Tommy's Bumper Sticker[2]

A little kid down at our church in Huntington Beach came up to me after he heard me talk about the Children's Free Enterprise Fund. He shook my hand and said, "My name is Tommy Tighe, I'm six years old and I want to borrow money from your Children's Fund."

I said, "Tommy, that's one of my goals, to loan money to kids. And so far all the kids have paid it back. What do you want to do?"

He said, "Ever since I was four, I had a vision that I could cause peace in the world. I want to make a bumper sticker that says, 'PEACE PLEASE! DO IT FOR US KIDS,' signed 'Tommy.' "

"I can get behind that," I said. He needed $454 to produce a thousand bumper stickers. The Mark Victor Hansen Children's Free Enterprise Fund wrote a check to the printer who was printing the bumper stickers.

Tommy's dad whispered in my ear, "If he doesn't pay the loan back, are you going to foreclose on his bicycle?"

I said, "No, knock on wood, every kid is born with honesty, morality and ethics. They have to be taught something else. I believe he'll pay us back." If you have a child who is over nine, let them w-o-r-k for m-o-n-e-y for someone honest, moral and ethical so they learn the principle early.

[2]Excerpted and used with permission from *Chicken Soup for the Soul: 101 Stories to Open the Heart and Rekindle the Spirit*, by Jack Canfield and Mark Victor Hansen (Deerfield Beach, FL: Health Communications, 1993).

We gave Tommy a copy of all of my tapes, and he listened to them twenty-one times each and took ownership of the material. It says, "Always start selling at the top." Tommy convinced his dad to drive him up to Ronald Reagan's home. Tommy rang the bell and the gatekeeper came out. Tommy gave a two-minute, irresistible sales presentation on his bumper sticker. The gatekeeper reached in his pocket, gave Tommy $1.50 and said, "Here, I want one of those. Hold on and I'll get the former President."

I asked, "Why did you ask him to buy?" He said, "You said in the tapes to ask everyone to buy." I said, "I did. I did. I'm guilty."

He sent a bumper sticker to Mikhail Gorbachev with a bill for $1.50 in U.S. funds. Gorbachev sent him back $1.50 and a picture that said, "Go for peace, Tommy," and signed it, "Mikhail Gorbachev, President."

Since I collect autographs, I told Tommy, "I'll give you $500 for Gorbachev's autograph."

He said, "No thanks, Mark."

I said, "Tommy, I own several companies. When you get older, I'd like to hire you."

"Are you kidding?" he answered. "When I get older, I'm going to hire you."

The Sunday edition of the *Orange County Register* did a feature section on Tommy's story, the Children's Free Enterprise Fund and me. Marty Shaw, the journalist, interviewed Tommy for six hours and wrote a phenomenal interview. Marty asked Tommy what he thought his impact would be on world peace. Tommy said, "I don't think I am old enough yet; I think you have to be eight or nine to stop all the wars in the world."

Marty asked, "Who are your heroes?"

He said, "My dad, George Burns, Wally Joiner and Mark Victor Hansen." Tommy has good taste in role models.

Three days later, I got a call from the Hallmark Greeting Card Company. A Hallmark franchisee had faxed a copy of the *Register* article. They were having a convention in San Francisco and wanted Tommy to speak. After all, they saw that Tommy had nine goals for himself:

1. Call about cost (baseball card collateral).
2. Have bumper sticker printed.
3. Make a plan for a loan.
4. Find out how to tell people.
5. Get address of leaders.
6. Write a letter to all of the presidents and leaders of other countries and send them all a free bumper sticker.
7. Talk to everyone about peace.
8. Call the newspaper stand and talk about my business.
9. Have a talk with school.

Hallmark wanted my company, Look Who's Talking, to book Tommy to speak. While the talk did not happen because the two-week lead time was too short, the negotiation between Hallmark, myself and Tommy was fun, uplifting and powerful.

Two years later, Joan Rivers called Tommy Tighe to be on her syndicated television show. Someone had also faxed her a copy of the *Register* interview on Tommy.

"Tommy," Joan said, "this is Joan Rivers and I want you on my TV show which is viewed by millions."

"Great!" said Tommy. He didn't know her from a bottle of Vicks.

"I'll pay you $300," said Joan.

"Great!" said Tommy. Having listened repeatedly to and mastered my *Sell Yourself Rich* tapes, Tommy continued selling Joan by saying, "I am only eight years old, so I can't come alone. You can afford to pay for my mom too, can't you, Joan?"

"Yes!" Joan replied.

"By the way, I just watched a 'Lifestyles of the Rich and Famous' show and it said to stay at the Trump Plaza when you're in New York. You can make that happen, can't you, Joan?"

"Yes," she answered.

"The show also said when in New York, you ought to visit the Empire State Building and the Statue of Liberty. You can get us tickets, can't you?"

"Yes . . ."

"Great. Did I tell you my mom doesn't drive? So we can use your limo, can't we?"

"Sure," said Joan.

Tommy went on "The Joan Rivers Show" and wowed Joan, the camera crew, the live and television audiences. He was so handsome, interesting, authentic and such a great self-starter. He told such captivating and persuasive stories that the audience was found pulling money out of their wallets to buy bumper stickers on the spot.

At the end of the show, Joan leaned in and asked, "Tommy, do you really think your bumper sticker will cause peace in the world?"

Tommy, enthusiastically and with a radiant smile, said, "So far I've had it out two years and got the Berlin Wall down. I'm doing pretty good, don't you think?"[3]

---

[3]To date Tommy has sold over 2,500 of his bumper stickers and has repaid his $454 grant to Mark Victor Hansen's Children's Free Enterprise Fund. If you'd like to order one of Tommy's bumper stickers, send $3.00 to Tommy Tighe, 17283 Ward Street, Fountain Valley, CA 92708.

If you know of enterprising teenagers who want grants, have them write letters to Mark explaining what they want the money for, how much they want and how they will pay it back.

For making this possible, and for all his other unselfish and innovative acts of philanthropy, we consider Del Smith to be the Andrew Carnegie of our time.

STEP 11

Go for King of the Mountain

We encourage you to aim high. Go for being "king of the mountain." It's a realistic dream because there are lots of mountains. There is a mountain for every man and woman alive.

One who did this was Dr. Robert Schuller. He had a dream. He wanted to build the Crystal Cathedral, an incredible church with thousands of square feet of windows, which would cost tens of millions of dollars. Everyone said it was impossible to achieve such a dream. But Dr. Schuller knew better. He wrote down his goal succinctly. Then he added a twist. He added ten outrageous solutions to it.

One of his solutions was to ask somebody to donate $1 million. People scoffed at the idea. But he went to John Crean, the owner of Fleetwood Industries (which manufactures mobile homes and recreational vehicles), and Crean just sat down and wrote out a check for $1 million. Crean then went on to raise almost $28 million more in donations for Schuller. Schuller's next outrageous solution was to have six more people give $1 million each. Well, John Wayne gave a million right before he died. Bob Hope gave a million. Rich DeVoss of Amway gave a million. When he talked to Clement Stone, Clem told him, "You get the other five, I'll give you the magic sixth." He did!

Yet another solution was to collect $1 million at a single Sunday service. At that time he only had a thousand people coming to the church on Sunday. That came to $1,000 a person. But he asked them all for it, and as unbelievable as it may seem, they gave a million at that Sunday service! He went right on down his list of outrageous solutions until the cathedral was built. The key that made it all possible was to go for the whole dream.

Another person who understood this principle was Dr. Paul Yongi Cho. He came here from Korea to study with Dr. Schuller. Then he went back to Korea to build his own church. He started with just three people in a hovel. But he didn't let his immediate circumstances stifle him. His dream was kingly. He wrote down that he would have 150 people attending services in a year and that in the second year he would double that! He visualized it and affirmed it to others. Today his church has over 1 million members. His church building seats eighty thousand. He has as many as ten services every Sunday. He dared to dream big, to be king of the mountain.

We've picked two examples of raising money for religious purposes, but the technique works just as well in the secular world. A number of years ago Kemmons Wilson was traveling through the South and noticed that there weren't any affordable places for families to stay. So he decided not to open a single hotel, but a chain of hotels. He founded Holiday Inns. From the beginning the Holiday Inn sign has proclaimed it "The World's Innkeeper." Well, in the years since then, that's just what it's become. Wilson built, and then sold, the world's largest hotel chain.

Remember, it doesn't cost any more to dream great dreams. So, as long as you're going for prosperity, aim to be "king of the mountain!" There are plenty of mountains, enough for everyone to be king or queen of one.

Setting Your Prosperity Goals

If you have trouble deciding what your prosperity goals should be, then interview yourself. Pretend you're Barbara Walters or Dan Rather. Here are some typical interview questions:

1. What am I waiting for?
2. What are my real talents?
3. Above all else, what would I really like to have and be?
4. What are my hobbies?
5. Would any of these lead to a vocation?
6. Do I really dare to take a risk?
7. If I did exactly what I wanted to do, what would it be?
8. What's stopping me from doing it now?
9. What are my greatest strengths (good with people, machines, numbers, etc.)?
10. With whom would I like to associate (teachers, executives, salespeople, sports figures, celebrities, etc.)?
11. Do I need to invest more in my training or education to advance to where I want to be?
12. Why am I not doing that now?
13. What are my great ideas?
14. Have I written them down?

STEP 12

Be Assertive in Your Actions

Once you've defined your goals, don't let anything stop you. Dr. Norman Vincent Peale tells the story of a young man eager to get a job during the Depression. He read a want ad that fitted his abilities perfectly and ran to the company, only to see thirty-seven men in line ahead of him. He could simply have stood in line and waited and probably been turned down. But instead he wrote the following note and handed it to the boss's secretary to hand to the boss, who was holding the interviews. It said simply, "Please don't hire anyone until you interview person #38, James Henry."

He went back in line. A few moments later the boss came out and ran down the line to him. He said, "Creativity and initiative are what I'm looking for. James, you're hired!"

9

Achieving Total Well-Being

It's never too late to rebuild a healthy life.

It's fun to be fit, to eat right and to discipline yourself to do these things. Do them for thirty days, says Dr. Maxwell Maltz, author of *Psycho-Cybernetics,* and they become a habit that's harder *not* to do on the thirty-first day than it is to do.

Most addictions are considered bad, but try to addict yourself to good habits. Create what Dr. William Glasser calls "positive addictions." With good diet and exercise—and the positive attitude that stems from that commitment—will come a new sense of well-being. Small illnesses will disappear and big ones diminish. Instead of having to focus so much energy on keeping well, on maintaining health, it will become second nature. Once we wake up to new levels of physicality, we wake up to new levels of emotionality, new levels of mentality, new levels of spirituality and on and on. Anytime we discipline one area of our lives, it cascades through all the other areas. Good health not only leads to a feeling of well-being, but also allows us to maintain a balance in our entire lives.

What Is Total Well-Being?

Total well-being can be defined as pursuing appropriate goals in all areas of our life. With regard to health, it's staying within our ideal body weight, experiencing sound nutrition, maintaining a systematic physical-fitness program, using stress-reduction techniques, having a sense of play in our outlook on life, learning how to increase our longevity and giving ourselves the reward of high-level freedom from pain.

What Do You Want?

We're not going to change our diet and add exercise to our regimen unless we see immediate personal benefits. So to begin, decide exactly what you want from it. Here are some suggestions. Do you want:

A trimmer, flatter stomach?
Rippling, well-defined muscles?
Freedom from smoking, drinking or drugs?
A lower heart rate?
A lower cholesterol level?
A lower fat intake?
A body in better condition?
More flexibility?
A much better internal feeling?

We all want one or more of the above. So what are you waiting for? What is the definition of well-being for you? Close your eyes and visualize your highest level of well-being. Write out what you see, feel and believe about wellness for you.

Choose at least one personal goal for enhanced well-being per month. Write it out on a card. Carry it in your pocket, next to your money. Review it daily. Meditate on the idea, working back from the desired end result. Ask yourself, "Is what I am doing today—now—moving me closer to the accomplishment of my desired objective?"

> *One psychiatric stress expert said with regard to well-being, "There are only two principles: (1) don't sweat the small stuff, and (2) everything is small stuff!"*

Measuring Your Health

There are many health measurements that can be taken by a physician to help determine how well you are. The following five—which you can do for yourself—will give you a good clue. Before embarking on any fitness program, of course, you should check with a physician and get his or her approval.

1. *What is your resting heart rate?* The lower it is, the better it is. Olympic athletes average as low as thirty-six beats per minute. Take your pulse at your neck, wrist or behind your knee. Ask a friend to help instruct you if you've never done it. For each of us, there is a first time and no need for embarrassment. Use a clock or watch with a sweeping second hand; there will be less room for error. Count your pulse beats for six seconds and multiply by ten; that's your heart rate. If your pulse rate is

seven beats in six seconds, multiply times ten: seventy beats a minute, which is average. The goal is to lower that rate, enabling yourself to live longer and healthier because the heart doesn't have to work as hard.

The best time to discover your resting pulse rate is just after a good night's rest, upon awakening and before getting out of bed. Most people are in the sixty to ninety range. If you're above eighty beats a minute and haven't visited a physician in the last year, go at once.

2. *What is your recovery rate?* Recovery heart rate is the number of minutes it takes you to get back to a resting heart rate after aerobic exercise—whether it be one, two, ten, fifteen or twenty minutes. The faster you recover, the more fit you are. Good aerobic teachers check their students to make sure they know and use all the common heart-rate measurements. You should make sure you learn from a pro. It could save your life or someone else's.

3. *What is your percentage of body fat?* Dr. David Starr, an Olympic sports-medicine chiropractor, says the definition of desirable weight is the weight at which we feel well, look well, are alert and resist fatigue and infection. He says we're overweight when we're 10 percent above our desirable weight.

A more accurate method is to determine the actual percentage of our body that is fat. The ideal for women is 23 percent and for men 15 percent body fat. Covert Bailey, author of *Fit or Fat,* is at the leading edge of this approach. He does underwater immersion at his seminars to maximize the accuracy of body-fat testing. Similar tests are now done in traveling mobile units, at YMCAs, health clubs and universities.

Occasionally doctors and nutritionists use a caliper to test body fat. Laypeople do the "pinch an inch" test for obesity. If you can pinch an inch or more of fat around your abdomen, on the bottom of the triceps—when the arm is bent skyward like a right-hand turn signal—or on your back, under the scapula, when your arm is bent behind your back as in a wrestler's hammerlock, you're too fat.

Being overweight is a serious problem. At Oral Roberts University, students are suspended if they are unfit and go above the range of their ideal body fat. We visited that campus and the Ken Cooper aerobics center at 5:30 P.M. on a Friday night and were amazed to find it packed with students, faculty and guests using all the facilities to the maximum—playing basketball, volleyball, swimming, running and weight lifting. It was an inspirational experience to observe.

4. *How flexible are you?* Can you comfortably touch your toes, do deep-knee bends and sit in yoga postures? To find out, gently and slowly try doing these things. If you find they're difficult or impossible to do, don't panic. No matter what your age, you can gently and progressively stretch and loosen yourself again.

5. *What is your fun level?* We all need play, laughter, whimsy, spontaneity—in other words, *fun*—in our lives. Are you getting enough? Fun constitutes exercise not only for the body, but for the mind as well. Laughter alone can give us a whole body exercise—and it can both relieve tension and revitalize us. The late Dr. Norman Cousins, in his two books, *Anatomy of an Illness* and *The Healing Heart*, demonstrates how he was pulled back from death by laughter (with some help from vitamin C). If we have excellent attitudes, then our lives will be filled with joyous laughter. If they aren't, then it's something we've got to work on.

Count how many times a day you have fun in one way

or another. If you can count ten separate incidents, you're doing great. If it's less than ten, you're deprived. You need to lighten up, be less serious and spend more time *having* a good time.

Getting Fit

If you take the above tests and find that you need some improvement, then the good news is that you're in the majority. Everyone wants to get fit, but somehow most of us never quite make it. If that's your problem, then here's a solution. It's our formula to Feel-Fit-Inside-So-It-Shows-Outside. Try it and you'll never let yourself go.

Get into Exercising

Dr. George Sheehan, the guru of runners and author of *Running and Being*, is a seventy-plus-year-old cardiologist who promotes exercise. He says that it integrates the body and soul into a holistic feeling of total wellness. It is an act, he feels, that brings together work, play, love and religion. "Fitness is imperative if we are to find ourselves, win self-respect and meet life's challenges."

> *"Man was not meant to be at rest. If fitness goes, can the mind be far behind?"*
> —DR. GEORGE SHEEHAN

Select an Exercise Program

The first step in getting fit is to select an exercise program. There are all sorts available, and most are excellent. Pick and choose from walking, jogging, roller skating, aerobics (watch Jane Fonda, Richard Simmons, Jack La Lanne or any of the other TV exercise gurus), treadmills, cross-country skiing, jumping rope, Nordic track or even trampolining (one of the most effective exercise techniques, according to the U.S. Air Force).

Exercise with Someone Else

Often it's possible to combine our exercise programs. We both exercise and run with our wives and children. We started jogging with our youngest children soon after their first birthdays, with them strapped into our snugglies, and later continued the practice, pushing the kids ahead of us in a three-wheeled jogging cycle. It's one of the more loving things you can do. Those of you who have spouses or sweethearts are encouraged to at least walk with that person half an hour a day for exercise. Apart from the health benefits to both of you, it will deepen the feeling of connection between you.

If there isn't an exercise partner available, use your imagination to create one. When we're on the road and our energy is lackluster, occasionally we'll fantasize that we're running with our friends, with each other or with celebrities we admire. It's possible even to have imaginary conversations that will help pick up your energy level as you run.

The ultimate exercise program, however, is to run with a group. One of our clients recently got us enthused about the Bay to Breakers run in San Francisco. Once a year, roughly 125,000 people run a marathon through the streets of downtown San Francisco out to the Pacific Ocean. Imagine running with 125,000 people!

> *"Get fit, then diet. Most people diet first, then exercise."*
> —COVERT BAILEY

Five Days to Fitness

Regardless of your program or with whom you do it, it's important to exercise at least three days a week for maintenance.

But five days a week will keep you totally fit. (In the beginning it's best to exercise more often, but in small amounts—perhaps ten minutes per session, twice a day—until you build up your muscles and stamina.) Also do compensating exercise; if you feel like taking a shorter exercise one day, take a longer one the next.

Aim for Aerobic Exercise

Aerobics is for the whole body. It means "with air"—oxygen in the lungs and blood vessels. Aerobics is steady, uninterrupted exercise demanding muscular output for twenty minutes or more. The most noticeable benefits of aerobics are increased energy and an overall feeling of well-being. Four times a week or more for twenty minutes or more a day will develop a fit cardiovascular-pulmonary system leading to life-long wellness.

> *"If marathoners finish, they win."*
> —DR. GEORGE SHEEHAN

Alternative Programs

If strenuous exercise is too difficult for you, try extended walks. If this can be done in a wilderness area, you'll get out of it both exercise and enjoyment of the beauty around you. Wilderness walks are especially therapeutic for anyone who's feeling depressed. If you can get away for a whole day or, better yet, hike for several days on a path such as the Appalachian or the John Muir Trail, you'll find it immensely invigorating.

Extensive barefoot walks on the beach are also enormously beneficial. Periodically try to schedule time alone for walking in the woods or barefoot on the beach. Remember, whatever you look at is what you internalize. So choose to look for beauty, awe and excitement rather than ugliness, pain and negativity.

Do It Regularly

Perhaps the most important part of your program should be its regularity—a daily regimen that supports your decision to get fit. The trouble is that most people say, "I would exercise, but I don't have the time." That, of course, is hogwash. We're both about as busy as anyone we know, and we run five days a week—usually in different time zones. We place exercise at the top of our agenda. Just as in gaining prosperity we need to take our profit out first, with fitness we need to take our exercise out first from our daily schedule.

If you have trouble rationalizing the importance of an exercise program in your daily schedule, just remember that every vital lifestyle and life agenda requires that we be totally fit and ready for anything. You could be in an auto crash. You could catch some disease. If you're fit, your chances of prevention are far higher, and so are your chances of survival and recovery.

Remember, to achieve regularity in our exercise activities, we must give ourselves support in terms of good reasons for doing it. If the reasons are either inviting enough or threatening enough, we'll do it.

The benefits of regular exercise include:

1. You feel better.
2. You think better.
3. You perform better.
4. You are psychologically uplifted.
5. You lower your heart rate and blood pressure.
6. You reduce your cholesterol level.
7. You increase high-density lipid proteins.
8. You live longer.
9. You have greater endurance.
10. You have reduced tension, depression, anxiety and other symptoms of stress.
11. You have higher self-esteem.

Make the Connection

Finally, associate your exercise program with your specific health goals. If your goal is to trim your waist, slowly increase your level of exercise until your waist goes down, and always keep track of your pulse. Avoid overly strenuous exercise, but do enough to remove that extra poundage and keep it off.

> *"To replace fat with muscle, exercise longer, not harder."*
>
> —COVERT BAILEY

Don't Over-Exercise

Virtually any exercise will raise the heartbeat. This is desirable, since it produces an aerobic effect that is valuable to our entire body. But we want to be careful not to overdo it. We don't want to get our heartbeat *too* high. Before starting any exercise, as we mentioned earlier, you should check with your physician for previously undiscovered illness or health risks. Once you start the program, you'll need to get your heartbeat up to a minimum level for the aerobic effect. One way you can use to arrive at that level is to subtract your age from 220 and multiply by 70 percent. This should equal the training effect. For example:

$$
\begin{array}{r}
220 \\
-\ 40 \\
\hline
180\% \\
\times\ 70 \\
\hline
\end{array}
$$

126 beats per minute during 20 minutes
of regular aerobic activity.

Another useful technique is the talk test. The talk test for heartbeat is used to set your pace. If you can talk comfortably to your partner while you're exercising, your heartbeat is probably okay. If you're too out of breath to converse, you're probably exercising too hard.

Don't Overeat

It will take thirty minutes of moderate aerobic dancing to burn off twelve to sixteen corn chips. If you run a ten-minute pace per mile for forty minutes, you can have a hot fudge sundae and stay even. A slice of blueberry pie is going to cost you thirty minutes of racquetball, according to the *New Guide to Fitness* by Dr. David Starr.

Being overweight is like having a knapsack of fat. A friend of ours, Pete Strudwick, once pointed out that if we're only one pound overweight and we run one mile, we've carried the equivalent of a ton of extra weight!

The average American male, weighing 180 pounds at age thirty, has 15 percent body fat (an ideal percentage). If he still weighs 180 pounds by the time he reaches the age of forty, he will probably have 40 percent body fat.

Does all this give you pause? It should.

The counterbalancing force is a sensible diet as well as a program of regular exercise. Since most people become more sedentary as they grow older, they need not only to get more exercise, but also to cut back further and further on calories as they maintain a balanced and moderate diet. The prototype older man, in our opinion, is Jack La Lanne. Yearly, he challenges a record. He still looks great, exercises two hours a day, eats perfectly, runs several profitable enterprises including fitness centers and has a popular TV show.

Rethinking Our Ideas About Food

When we were children, we were told to clean our plates. "There are starving children in China" was the warning. But eating the plate clean never fed anyone but us. The point is that nearly all of us bring from childhood a program of compulsive eating. To diet we need to reprogram, re-think and re-feel our way through food, meals and nutrition.

First, we need to ask ourselves, "Why am I eating? Is it because I'm really hungry? Or is it to satisfy something else, perhaps an emotional need?" Every time you eat, consider your hunger on a scale of one to ten. What is your emotion at the time? What's your real reason for eating?

Next, we need to face facts with regard to calories. Too often we blame our excess weight on binges. We feel that in general we eat a good diet, but once in a while we binge, and that's what adds weight to our bodies. Not true. People who say after a holiday binge, "I gained five pounds over the weekend" are either kidding themselves or don't know what they're talking about. Since one pound of fat represents 3,500 calories of intake, to gain five pounds would mean consuming 17,500 calories over a single weekend. Impossible. That gain came from a long-term pattern of overeating.

Remember, if you eat an extra 100 calories a day over one year, you will gain ten pounds. Your body is like a bank that works on the basis of deposits and withdrawals.

Finally, we need to avoid the mind-set that tells us we need to lose a lot of weight quickly. Remember, if someone has a large weight loss in a short period of time, it's mostly water loss. (To lose just 1,500 calories a day requires one-and-a-half hours of jogging at 6.5 miles per hour.)

> *Smart people start their diet at the supermarket. You can't eat what you don't buy.*

Fad Diets

Fad diets don't work. Statistics indicate that they are less than 5 percent successful. They usually result in the "Ping-Pong" effect. We go on a diet and lose again, gain it back and go on a diet again, and so forth. Fad diets are usually the domain of "professional" dieters, people who actually lose thousands of pounds in the course of a lifetime, and gain them all back again. Medical science indicates that this can be extremely stressful and harmful to the body.

Diuretics also result in an immediate loss of weight. But it's all water. The fat remains. Diet pills take off some weight too, but their chances of causing harm usually outweigh any small benefit they may offer.

Maintain It, Don't Regain It

The real objective is a sensible lifelong plan of diet and exercise. Remember, it's much easier and more effective to maintain your good health than to regain it once it's lost.

If your stomach could talk to us, chances are it would say, "I just digest it—you eat it." When we control our appetite, we control our lives. The trouble is that most of us allow our taste buds to control our eating and, hence, our lives.

The notion of a nutritious diet is defeated at every turn. Our top athletes and actors teach our kids to eat junk food on TV. There are an estimated seven thousand junk-food commercials currently on the market. Even the heroes of our culture are involved. Bill Cosby sells Coca-Cola and Jello, while Michael Jordan hypes for McDonald's.

Eat a sensible, well-thought-out diet one day at a time. Here are some tips on getting started:

1. Decrease surplus food at meals.
2. Don't snack at all. It weakens discipline.
3. If you must snack, avoid all high-calorie snacks.
4. Avoid socializing in eating areas (except family dinner). This will just stimulate your appetite.
5. Avoid TV commercials—most are about food.
6. Avoid sugar, white flour and salt.

7. Eat slowly. You'll get filled up in about twenty minutes *regardless* of how little you eat.
8. Visualize your fitness many times each day. Imagine a picture of yourself at your ideal weight. Or better still, get a photo of yourself when you looked that way and review it at least three times daily.
9. Each time you start to eat something, imagine your ideal weight and ask yourself, "Will this help me to achieve and maintain my ideal weight?" If the answer is no, don't eat it.

Dr. David Starr says the overeating cycle goes from stress to compulsive eating and/or drinking to obesity to physical inactivity to more stress. It's a self-sabotaging cycle that only your decision, desire, determination and dedication can break.

You create your own fitness. Your diet will quite literally determine the length and enjoyment of your life.

Fat is the symptom of being overweight, not the cause.

Work from the Desired Result

Remember, our lifelong objective is our total well-being, not just the absence of sickness and disease. Michael Wickett, a professional speaker, says, "Let *results* be your guru." You know what you really believe not by words but *deeds*. If you say you want to lose weight, your subconscious believes only your activities, not your intentions. Are you thinking fit, eating less and exercising more? The truth of your *belief* is visible in the results.

Affirm It

Here are a series of health affirmations that you can use to motivate yourself. Make a point of saying them often—particularly before, during and after exercise:

1. I am responsible for my good health.
2. My daily habits *create* my good health.
3. I am vibrantly healthy in spirit, mind and body.
4. I am totally well and staying that way all the days of my life!
5. I feel totally alive and inspire others to feel the same way!

Get a Support System

Achieving wellness is a long road and it requires a considerable amount of support. Developing a support system along the way should be a prime consideration. You should look for fit friends who tell you that they're ready, willing and able to support you to the "max." You should seek an attractive environment for your energized activities.

Until you've got your own fitness story to tell, listen to others and improvise your own, using your "inner ear." In your mind, hear people telling you, "You look great! You're a shadow of your former self. You look younger now that you've lost weight!" Hear your M.D. say, "You're at your ideal body weight, with a perfect pulse rate. You're in perfect shape. It's a new you—congratulations!" It will delight you months in the future when they actually say it to you. Only you will know you put the words in their mouths.

Exercise Is "In"

If you still have any doubts, remember that in the sixties it was estimated that less than 25 percent of the U.S. population regularly engaged in strenuous physical activity. In the nineties, over 60 percent of Americans are involved in some kind of fitness program. It has become the fashionable thing to do no matter what your age or sex. Sweat is *in*. So you couldn't be picking a better time to be getting into shape. You'll have lots of good company for many more years.

Health Healing

Everything we've said thus far relating to health has been preventative in nature. But sometimes we do get ill, and then we need some other kind of treatment. Until the late 1970s the *only* kind of treatment available for most of us was curative in nature. We would walk into a doctor's office, and he or she would ask, "What's your problem?" As soon as we explained what it was, we'd be offered pills, shots or surgery. Now, however, there are other alternatives, and one of them is health healing.

Today, around the world, there are hundreds of thousands of people born with natural healing powers and the "healing touch." They are part of every race; creed, color or finances don't affect their natural ability. The real loss is that many of us have the power to be natural "healing channels," yet we have never recognized or even tried our possible talent. We encourage everyone to see if they have the gift of healing.

Dr. Olga Worral, now deceased, was one of the greatest natural healers. She said, "My research shows that everyone has some natural healing power, and 5 percent of us have outstanding abilities. If you are part of the 5 percent, you were born to heal yourself and others."

Real healers like E. G. "Ted" Fricker of London, say, "I can heal skeptics, unbelievers and those whose faith has been shattered by long bouts with disease. You don't have to have any faith. I have enough for both of us.

Mark's Experience

"I was appearing at a meeting in Columbia, Missouri, and the night before, because of a back problem, I couldn't sleep. So at six o'clock in the morning I called for help. I could barely move in the bed and every time I moved, I had extraordinary pain.

"Through the kind services of one of the sponsors of the program, I immediately got in to see an orthopedic surgeon, who did a whole series of tests, took X rays, then came back and said, 'You've got a degenerative disk in your spine. At the very least you need to go into traction immediately, but that probably won't work. Actually, we should operate as soon as possible.'

"Now, I don't like invasive surgery, so I asked for a second opinion. The doctor said, 'The only thing I can do for you is give you codeine to relieve the pain.' I talked with six other doctors with no more satisfaction. I flew to New Mexico for acupuncture. I went to see a neurologist, an orthopedist, three chiropractors and every kind of back doctor, and the diagnosis always seemed to be the same.

"Finally I took a few days off at my condo in Hawaii, and because I'm willing to experiment with almost anything that doesn't involve drugs or surgery, a lady at our condo put me in touch with one of the high kahunas who do faith healing. At our first meeting, which was short, he told me that I had to watch the sun go down and release every negative word, thought and deed into the dying light. (This is similar to what Christians call repentance.)

"I did, and the next day he came back and gave me a deep structural massage which was similar to 'rolfing.' We got to talking about India, and he asked me if, when I was there, I had heard about Kundalini, a yoga technique that involves taking very deep breaths to put one 'in concert with the energy of the universe.' I replied that I had heard of it.

"He took me through an exercise in Kundalini power. It was a deep meditative trance. He put me through controlled Kundalini in and out and through my body and my spine and into my degenerative disk. He said, 'You'll see colors and you'll see it glow and then regrow.'

"The entire process took six hours. When I was finished, it *was* regenerated, healed. When new X rays were taken, they showed no degenerative disk. The medical doctors couldn't believe it. They said a disk can't regenerate. Once it's gone, it's gone. It was a medical miracle. It really wasn't; it's just that their version of the truth didn't apply in my case. The medical model comes from curative rather than regenerative medicine. I wanted to be healed, I believed I would be healed, so I was healed."

Jack's Experience

"I was swimming with friends in a small pond in Western Massachusetts. As I was getting out of the water, I stepped on a broken bottle at the bottom of the pond. It put a deep three-inch gash in the instep of my foot. It was bleeding profusely. It was a long walk from the pond back to the main highway where our cars were parked, so I decided to use a self-healing technique I had read about in a book by Oregon healer Dr. Jack Schwartz.

"I wrapped a towel tightly around my foot to help stop the bleeding. I then closed my eyes and went into the deepest state of relaxation and concentration I could muster under the circumstances. I then visualized a three-dimensional mirror image of myself sitting opposite me. I then expanded that image until it was about as big as the statue of Abraham Lincoln at the Lincoln Memorial in Washington, D.C.

"I then imagined walking over to the 'statue' of Jack Canfield and found a door in the side that said 'Maintenance Room.' I went in, took out chicken wire, cement, paint and a variety of tools. I then went to the cut foot, patched it with chicken wire, covered it with cement and plaster, watched it dry and painted it until it looked like the rest of the human statue of Jack. Next I put the tools away, closed the door and sat back down inside myself. Finally, I shrank the statue back down to normal size and imagined rejoining with it, becoming me again in my mind.

"This whole process took about fifteen to twenty minutes. When I opened my eyes and looked at my foot, the bleeding had stopped and there was no scab. There was just a little flap of clean skin there. The deep cut had miraculously closed itself. I proceeded to walk the three-quarters of a mile back to the road. I limped slightly but the cut did not reopen. The next day, I played volleyball barefoot!

"A doctor who had been part of our group told me that he was truly amazed. He said that normally such a cut would take five stitches and days to repair itself. It is truly amazing what our bodies can do when the healing powers and energies of the mind and spirit are properly used."

We're not recommending these techniques to anyone in place of medical attention. You and your doctor need to make these determinations. But you should be aware that there are alternatives to surgery and the curative concept of medicine. In most cases all that's required is for us to expand our level of consciousness, to change the way we think in order to change the way we feel.

Aim for Total Well-Being

As we mentioned at the beginning of this chapter, health is only one element of well-being, albeit a most important one. Good health allows us to balance our lives, gives us the energy to move toward prosperity, to give and receive love, to enhance our mental, social and spiritual growth.

We'd like to conclude this chapter with the true story of Patti Wilson of Orange County, California. At a young and tender age, Patti was told by her doctor that she was an epileptic. Her father, Jim Wilson, is a morning jogger, and one day she smiled through her teenage braces and said, "Daddy, what I'd *really* love to do is run with you every day. But I'm afraid I'll have a seizure."

Her father told her, "If you do, I know how to handle it. So let's start running!"

That's just what they did, every day. It was a wonderful experience for them to share, and there were no seizures at all while she was running. After a few weeks, she told her father, "Daddy, what I'd *really* love to do is break the world's long-distance running record for women."

Her father checked the *Guinness Book* and found that the farthest any woman had ever run was eighty miles. Patti thought about that a long time. Then, as a freshman in high school, she announced, "I'm going to run from Orange County up to San Francisco." (A distance of four hundred miles!) "As a sophomore," she went on, "I'm going to run to Portland, Oregon." (Over fifteen hundred miles!) "As a junior, I'll run to St. Louis." (About two thousand miles) "As a senior I'll run to the White House." (More than three thousand miles away!)

In view of her handicap, Patti was being as ambitious as she was enthusiastic. But she said she looked at the handicap of being an epileptic as simply "an inconvenience." She focused not on what she had lost but on what she had *left*.

That year she completed her run to San Francisco wearing a T-shirt that read, "I Love Epileptics." Her dad ran at her side, every mile. And her mom, a nurse, followed in a motor home behind them in case anything went wrong. Talk about high-quality family relationships!

In her sophomore year, Patti's classmates got behind her. They built a giant poster that read, "Run, Patti, Run!" (This has since become her motto and the title of a book she's written.) But on her second marathon, en route to Portland, she fractured a bone in her foot. A doctor told her she had to stop her run. He said, "I've got to put a cast on your ankle so that you don't sustain permanent damage."

She said, "Doc, you don't understand. This isn't just a whim of mine. It's a magnificent obsession! I'm not just doing it for me, I'm doing it to break the chains on the brains that limit so many others. Isn't there a way I can keep running?"

He gave her one option. He could wrap the ankle in adhesive. It would be incredibly painful. "And," he told her, "it will blister." She told the doctor to wrap it up.

She finished the run to Portland, completing her last mile with the governor of Oregon. You may have seen the headlines, "Super Runner Patti Wilson Ends Marathon For Epilepsy On Her 17th Birthday."

After four months of almost continuous running, Patti went to Washington and shook the hand of the president of the United States. She told him, "I wanted people to know that epileptics are normal human beings with normal lives."

Mark told this story at one of his seminars not long ago, and afterward a big teary-eyed man came up to him and stuck out his meaty hand and said, "My name is Jim Wilson. You were talking about my daughter, Patti." He told Mark that because of her noble efforts enough money had been raised to open up nineteen multimillion-dollar epileptic centers around the country.

If Patti Wilson can do so much with so little, what can you do to outperform yourself in a state of total wellness?

It's Who You Meet That Counts

"Five years from now, you'll be the same person you are today except for the people you meet, the books you read, the tapes you hear."
—CHARLES "TREMENDOUS" JONES

The people you meet should excite you, inspire you, make you grow. That's why you should endeavor constantly to add to the number and variety of people you meet. Each one will polish a different facet of your mind and stimulate you in ways you may not anticipate.

One of the people Mark always wanted to meet was Red Skelton. One day he was waiting in a lounge at an airport and he saw Red sitting there. Knowing that he was a superstar, Mark might have been intimidated and might not have found the courage to go and speak to him. Or having found the courage, he might have only gone up, bumbled a few words, asked for an autograph and left. But Red Skelton was one of the people he had long ago determined he was going to meet someday. He had written his name down on a list. So in his mind he *knew* that sooner or later he was going to meet and learn from him. Consequently, he had no trouble walking up and introducing himself.

"Mr. Skelton," he said, "you don't know me, but I'm a fan of yours."

"It's been a hot day," he replied. "I need a fan."

At first Mark was taken aback by his humor. Then he played to it. He said, "Mr. Skelton, is it true that you have a photographic memory?"

He said, "Yes, it's underdeveloped."

Within a few minutes they were laughing and talking like old pals. Mark spent an hour and a half with him. They talked about a lot of things, one of which related to broadcasting. Mark explained that he had been asked to do a couple of TV pilots for Public Broadcasting.

Red said that was great, but that when it came time to sign the contract, he should always hold out for the broadcast rights. They might not be worth anything immediately, but in the future they could be of sizable value.

Mark subsequently did the shows for Public Broadcasting. When he signed the contract, he made sure he retained all broadcast rights. Soon after, PBS discovered that it had lost all the money it thought it would have for those shows because Ronald Reagan pulled the plug on $160 million of its funding. Because Mark had the rights, a quarter-million dollars' worth of filming was turned over to him—for no charge!

Now Mark uses that film as invaluable promotional material.

You see, it wasn't that Mark was any particular kind of smart guy, it was his meeting with Red Skelton that gave him an insight based on Skelton's experience. It allowed him to grow and profit in the future.

Write It Down

It's one thing to think about meeting someone. It's quite another to write it down. As we've seen, writing down makes it a commitment. It tells our conscious mind what we want to do and puts the subconscious on notice that it had better get started figuring out how. (To further stimulate our subconscious, we can write out ten questions that we plan to ask the people we intend to meet.)

Aim to Meet Many Kinds of People

Meeting people who have lived very different lives will enrich you immensely. In our own experience, this came home to us when we met John Goddard, the real-life "Indiana Jones."

John is one of the world's great explorers and adventurers. At the age of fifteen he wrote a "Life List" of 127 goals, which included exploring the Nile, Amazon and Congo rivers, climbing Mount Everest and Mount Kilimanjaro, riding on an elephant, ostrich and bronco and retracing Marco Polo's travels. It also included reading the Bible, all of Shakespeare, Plato and Aristotle and an entire encyclopedia. He also wrote that he wanted to write a book and visit every country in the world.

At the age of sixty-eight, John has achieved 114 of his goals and is vigorously moving forward to accomplish the rest of what he set out to do at the age of fifteen. (Of course, he has been constantly adding to his list during the intervening years.) Interestingly, his goal #125, written at the age of fifteen, was to visit the moon. His vision and the world's technologies are coming together so that even this goal might yet be achieved!

John is far more adventurous than we are. We tend to have certain fears about going into unexplored territories. We would never do it on our own. Recently John called and asked Mark to go on an eight-mile hike into Santa Anita Canyon, a place that almost nobody has visited. The invitation came because Mark had expanded his social contacts to include people of great repute, such as John. He never would have dreamed of going himself, but because John called, Mark went.

Eighteen would-be adventurers gathered at John's ranch-style home in a Los Angeles suburb. After a quick and illuminating sight-seeing tour of his home (which is like a museum and includes one-of-a-kind relics, scriptures and artifacts), they started out.

They all introduced themselves and discovered that the one thing they all had in common was that they were friends of John. Each of the eighteen turned out to be so exciting and stimulating that even before they began, they had eighteen new contacts to polish their mental facets and inspire them.

The first part of the hike was a breeze. John talked of former experiences on these trails, starting from his childhood. After lunch at a mountain spring, John said, "We can climb up either this side of the mountain or that side."

Mark looked up, and both sides looked sheer. He thought John was joking, so he commented to his friend Mary, "You're a great swimmer, so why don't you swim up the waterfall?" Everyone laughed. Then they started up the vertical face of the mountain—without any rappeling gear.

John said simply, "Just follow me. Step where I step." Loren, a fifty-two-year-old stuntman who had gone for thirty-three years without an accident, followed the group to insure their safety.

Up the mountain they went, climbing virtually straight up. As Mark felt his heart racing, he realized that had he known beforehand what was involved, he would never have considered coming. But if he hadn't known John Goddard, he wouldn't have been invited.

The last three feet Mark was pulled over the top of a precipice by two assistants. He felt renewed, exhilarated, exalted. He had made it.

It turned out to be only a resting point before they moved on. John then asked them individually to think of their most thrilling experience, their greatest adventure, to be retold at their next rest area. Mary declared, "This trip is it!"

They moved forward through deep brush and at one point had to cut away dense underbrush and crawl on hands and knees.

"Rough spots ahead," John would say periodically as they scaled another cliff and walked through rattlesnake-infested country. (At one point he snatched a five-foot bullhead snake out of a bush less than a foot in front of Mark!)

They saw signs of a recent coyote, a black bear and a deer. They walked under majestic two-hundred-year-old pine trees. At the next rest, John had them close their eyes and listen to the wilderness for three minutes and report on their powers of focus, concentration and observation. Amazingly, he recounted the sounds of six different kinds of bugs and birds.

When they finally returned, Mark felt he had had the experience of a lifetime. Not one to ever let things rest, John invited him to go through Yellowstone the following winter with him—on a dogsled!

If Mark hadn't had the Santa Anita Canyon experience, he would be less of a person today. If he hadn't expanded his circle of friends, he wouldn't have known John Goddard, and would not have been invited.

Since that time John has inspired both of us to set bigger and bolder goals.

Meeting Your Idol

It isn't necessary to eliminate "unlikely" people from the list of those you want to meet. The entire world is open to us. We can meet *anyone* we really want to meet. But unless we first put the name on our list, our chances of running into that person are remote.

Ten years ago Mark wrote down that he wanted to meet Dr.

Billy Graham. He isn't someone you are likely to run into, or the kind of person you can call up and say, "Billy, when you're in town, let's have lunch." He is, after all, the best-known evangelist in the world, according to *The Saturday Evening Post*. At one time he addressed one million people, live, in Korea. In his seventies, he is still actively "about his father's business," ministering to millions on national prime-time TV shows, writing a new book every year and involved in the numerous activities of his Minneapolis crusade committee.

Remember: whoever you are ready to meet is someone ready to meet you.

How to meet Dr. Graham? Mark left this challenge to his subconscious "inner knower" and wrote out simply that he wanted to meet Billy Graham.

Within a year he met him—in a fun and fulfilling way. This, in spite of the fact that everyone had told him it was impossible.

It occurred near John Wayne Airport in Newport Beach, California, close to Mark's home. Mark was with his wife, Patty, and they were scheduled to fly out for a speaking engagement. When they arrived at the airport, they learned that it was to be closed for an hour and a half. No reason was given.

They chose to spend an hour at Delaney's, a nearby restaurant with great food. While they were eating, Carol Brown, assistant head of the FAA, who helps run air activities at the airport, entered the dining room. They asked her to join them and then inquired why the airport was closed.

Carol explained that "Billy Graham is flying in, and there has been a threat to his life. Security is beefed up and we're temporarily rerouting traffic."

Immediately Mark asked, "Carol, can we meet him?" She

shook her head, but said, "I'll introduce you to the head of security."

Soon after, they were escorted to the security area, where there were perhaps twenty tough-looking, armed security men. They all seemed nervous, particularly the head of security, whose job it was to protect Dr. Graham. He flatly denied Mark's request.

But Mark wasn't going to let policy interfere with destiny.

He watched from inside the terminal as Dr. Graham exited the commercial airplane on which he was traveling. He was tall, tanned, elegant and poised, although the other passengers were seemingly unaware of this famous personage traveling in their midst (perhaps because he was wearing thick sunglasses and a gray cap).

The security guards enveloped him, and he was walked to a caravan of ordinary station wagons. Curiously, most of the security team then departed, presumably to get his baggage. Mark seized the opportunity.

In a pleasant and friendly way, Mark approached Dr. Graham with his hand extended to clasp his. His personal charisma, charm and radiance were immediately in evidence.

They began to talk, and Mark asked Dr. Graham the questions he had formulated in his mind over the years each time he had gone back and reread his name on his list. Dr. Graham cheerfully answered them all and had many of his own questions for Mark. They talked for a good time before Dr. Graham departed.

Our point is that Mark would never have dared to go up to meet Dr. Graham the way he did, or if he had gone, he wouldn't have known what to say, if nearly a decade earlier he hadn't written his name down on his list of people to meet.

Our Lists of People to Meet

We are so inspired by the idea of writing down people to meet that we've created sublists for people in different fields. Every time we meet one, after the name on our list we write, "Victory!" As you'll see by our lists, we haven't met everyone yet. Here are some names from our combined lists:

Authors

1. Og Mandino   *Victory!*
2. Michael LeBoeuf   *Victory!*
3. Jerry Gillies   *Victory!*
4. Don Dible   *Victory!*
5. Ram Dass   *Victory!*
6. Dr. Elisabeth Kubler-Ross   *Victory!*
7. Howard Fast
8. Sidney Sheldon
9. Robert Fulghum   *Victory!*
10. James Michener
11. Dr. Wayne Dyer   *Victory!*
12. Dr. Denis Waitley   *Victory!*
13. Dan Kennedy   *Victory!*
14. Dr. William Parker   *Victory!*
15. Dr. Jean Houston   *Victory!*
16. Judith Krantz
17. Shakti Gawain   *Victory!*
18. Richard Bach
19. Ken Keyes   *Victory!*
20. Harvey Diamond   *Victory!*

Speakers

1. Cavett Robert   *Victory!*
2. Zig Ziglar   *Victory!*
3. Mike Vance
4. Dr. Peter Drucker
5. Jim Rohn   *Victory!*
6. Dr. Norman Vincent Peale   *Victory!*

7. John Goddard   *Victory!*
8. Chip Collins   *Victory!*
9. Dr. Gunther Klaus
10. Ira Hayes   *Victory!*
11. Dr. Robert Schuller   *Victory!*
12. Danielle Kennedy   *Victory!*
13. Somers White   *Victory!*
14. Art Buchwald
15. Erma Bombeck
16. Patricia Fripp   *Victory!*
17. Jesse Jackson   *Victory!*
18. Bill Gore   *Victory!*
19. Earl Nightingale   *Victory!*
20. Dr. Leo Buscaglia   *Victory!*

Businesspeople

1. Wally "Famous" Amos   *Victory!*
2. Peter Ueberroth   *Victory!*
3. Peter Thomas   *Victory!*
4. Donald Trump
5. Peter Daniels   *Victory!*
6. W. Clement Stone   *Victory!*
7. Joe Gandolfo   *Victory!*
8. Lee Iacocca
9. Richard DeVoss
10. Mary Kay Ash   *Victory!*
11. Del Smith   *Victory!*
12. T. Boone Pickens
13. Venita Van Kaspel
14. Sam Curtis   *Victory!*
15. Byron Booth   *Victory!*
16. David Rockefeller
17. Stephen Jobs
18. Markita Andrews   *Victory!*

19. Ginny Sayer
20. Dr. Berny Jensen

Entertainers and Politicians

1. Della Reese   *Victory!*
2. Dr. David Viscott   *Victory!*
3. Johnny Carson
4. Bob Hope   *Victory!*
5. David Pomeranz   *Victory!*
6. Robert Redford
7. Red Skelton   *Victory!*
8. Oprah Winfrey   *Victory!*
9. Art Linkletter   *Victory!*
10. Garth Brooks
11. Pierce Brosnan   *Victory!*
12. Sidney Poitier   *Victory!*
13. Raquel Welch   *Victory!*
14. Bill Cosby   *Victory!*
15. Dr. Henry Kissinger
16. Dick Gregory   *Victory!*
17. Jane Fonda
18. Phil Donahue
19. Larry King
20. Steven Spielberg

Starting Your List

Write numbers sequentially from 1 to 100 on a blank piece of paper. Begin with any name that enters your head. Perhaps you'll jot down celebrities from TV, movies or music. You may add a who's who from local or national politics. Later, as you read your favorite magazines and books, other names will start looming up—people you'd like to meet in your own field of endeavor or areas of special interest.

Remember, your purpose here is to enrich and enliven yourself with what you learn from meeting the people on the list. You'll learn their goals, values, beliefs, doubts and fears, and this will awaken you to new levels of previously undiscovered potential in yourself. Your imagination will come alive with possibilities, and a new sense of excitement will pervade your thinking. You'll find yourself saying, "If they did it, so can I!"

Meeting Those on Your List

The law of attraction states that you will experience whatever you are thinking about long enough and deeply enough. If your goal is to meet someone, he or she will be there for you to meet. The law will bring you together; what you do with the opportunity is up to you.

Strengthening Your Mind

It's more dangerous to feed junk TV and newspapers to our minds than it is to feed junk food to our bodies.

We all have eighteen billion brain cells just raring to go, but how many of them do we actually use? Scientists tell us that we actually use only 10 percent of our mental capacity. Think how much more we could accomplish if we could just tap into that other 90 percent!

"Maybe I do have a big part of my brain that I'm not using," you may be saying, "but how do I access it? How do I get it to work for me?"

That's the subject of this chapter. We'll see how to put our minds to work toward achieving whatever it is we want.

Have a Purpose

We've already talked about the need to have a purpose in our lives. Let's expand on that a bit. A purpose is like the North Star, a guiding light that sets us on a course and keeps us fixed on it. Our minds need a purpose, or else we wander and drift, accomplishing little. Without a purpose, our achievements seem hollow, our future uncertain, our present chaotic. With a purpose, however, everything falls into place. We suddenly have a basis for making life decisions. Determining our purpose, therefore, should be our first mental task.

Here is a technique for finding out what your purpose in life may be. It was written by Vern Black, author of *Love Me, Love Myself.*

Our goal is to answer this question: "My purpose in life is to _____ people."

To answer this question, Bob suggests that we choose one of the following verbs to fill in the blank:

assist	inspire
facilitate	enroll
support	expand
serve	enable
stimulate	liberate
validate	guide
acknowledge	empower
discover	prepare
promote	enhance
organize	refine
strengthen	influence
cause	elevate

Once we finish this first step, we should have a pretty good general idea of what our purpose in life may be. Now we need to refine it. Here is the matrix:

	Describe the action you can see yourself doing for others	Describe the type of person you want to serve	Describe the goal you want to co-create with that person
My purpose in life is to	_____	_____	_____

We now fill in the blanks, trying to expand on the first sentence that we created. Here are some examples:

My purpose in life is to	Help	All People	Self-Actualize

My purpose in life is to	Expand	Children's	Ability to be happy
Mark Victor Hansen's purpose in life is to	Enlighten, Entertain, Inform, Educate, Empower, Enliven	As many people as possible	To dare to become winners

Jack Canfield's purpose in life is to	Inspire, empower	People	To live their highest vision in a context of love and joy

What's your purpose in life? Fill in the blanks and find out.

A Method for Increasing Mental Strength

Once we know our purpose, we can move forward in all areas—but especially in the mental. The mind is what directs us, so the mental is the most critical area to our achieving whatever results we want. Here are six steps you can take to help accomplish them:

STEP 1

Read Right

Will Rogers said, "I only know what I read in the papers." Think how sad a statement that is. For the most part, newspapers only print bad news. When was the last time you read something uplifting, inspiring and wonderful in the papers? It just isn't there. Unless it's bad news, editors and reporters say it's no news.

That's why it behooves us to read something else. (If you insist on reading newspapers, at least don't read them right before you go to bed, when they can cloud your mind with negative thoughts through the entire night!) Read books, good books. Those who have a purpose devour books that will lead them to achieving their goals. We all instinctively know that leaders are readers.

A person who can read and doesn't is no better than one who cannot read.

Jim Rohn, a motivational speaker in the business field, advocates that to be high achievers, we should make it a discipline to read two books a week. That averages out at about a hundred books a year. He quips, "If you've done that for the last ten years, you're a thousand books ahead. If you haven't, you're a thousand books behind."

```
┌─────────────────────────────────────┐
│              STEP 2                  │
└─────────────────────────────────────┘
```

Be a Mind Sharer

There are two elements to this step. The first is learning to read not only books but *people*. If we can master the art of reading people, our fortunes will have been half-made. The more we consciously observe people, the sooner we will discern habit patterns that predict future behavior. It doesn't matter what business we may be in. We are all in the people business.

The second element is *sharing* with those people who, after we read them, we judge to be empathetic and sympathetic to us. We call this *masterminding*. Masterminding involves meeting regularly with either another person or, preferably, a group of people, both as a support group and as an idea group. We challenge one another's thoughts. We push others' mental abilities. They, in turn, do the same for us. As a result, everyone grows mentally.

When we have a mastermind experience, and we are in rapport with other people, our mental power and strength explodes. Suddenly we become invincible because of the support of the others.

Mark formed his first real mastermind relationship in New York when he was twenty-six years old. He had just gone bankrupt. He got together with his insurance agent, a director of Chase Manhattan Bank, a real estate investor, a minister with a church of five thousand, a yogi and a salesman from American Medical Supply. They met every Thursday morning at 7:30 A.M. to launch themselves for the next week. They read the principles of *Think and Grow Rich*. They cheered one another on. They shared leads, shared business ideas and helped each other through.

> *You can train your mind to be magnetized to self-confidence, success and prosperity.*

Different people, while they were walking out, would grab one another's shirtsleeves and say, "Can I join you? I don't know what you're doing, but you sure feel good about doing it."

Don't Be Afraid of Sharing

Some of us are under the mistaken impression that there's only so much mind power to go around, that if we share some of ours with others, then it's our loss and their gain. Don't believe it for a moment.

Helen Keller said, "If you're in the dark, light your candle from mine. It will bring you light, and it doesn't diminish mine in any way." Even more to the point, Helen Kromer wrote a poem that addresses this directly:

> One mind awake can awaken another.
> The second awake can awaken their next-door brother.
> Three awake can awaken the town
> By turning the whole place upside down.
> Many awake can make such a fuss
> That they finally awaken the rest of us.

STEP 3

Become a "Mentee"

A "mentee" is one who studies under a mentor. If you want to improve your mind, then pick the best teachers. Listen to what they say and follow their lead.

We can't stress this enough. Bucky Fuller was Mark's mentor, and he learned more about life from him than he can say. Had he been less a person, he would have learned less. Fuller was a Renaissance man, a Leonardo da Vinci type, a genius and thinker par excellence.

How do we find great teachers? One way is to meet those super-achievers, those superstars whom we want to emulate. When we meet them, we should ask them who *their* teachers were. Invariably they will pass along the names, and they will often describe the tremendous impact these teachers have had on their lives.

There are all sorts of great opportunities to find good mentors. If you don't have access to someone personally, then there are other opportunities. Dr. Robert Schuller, for example, offers "Possibility Thinkers" luncheons. Motivational seminars are given by many organizations. There are always some going on regardless of where you live. We encourage you to attend at least one a month.

The great mentors are always traveling across the country talking to people. When they're in your area, make it your business to hear them. Here's a partial list of those we recommend:

Sheila Murray Bethel
John Bradshaw
Dr. Leo Buscaglia
Dr. Deepak Chopra
Dr. Barbara De Angelis
Dr. Wayne Dyer
Jerry Gillies
John Goddard
Dr. Louise Hay
Dr. Chris Hegarty
Og Mandino
Dan McBride

Terry McBride
Harvey McKay
Bob Proctor
Mark Rhode
Naomi Rhode
Tony Robbins
Cavett Robert
Jim Rohn
Dr. Robert Schuller
Marshall Thurber
Brian Tracy
Dr. Denis Waitley
Joel Weldon
Zig Ziglar

Each of these speakers has a different theme, whether it be motivation or business success or love or some other. But regardless of their particular topic, what they have in common is their ability to uplift you, to inspire you, to bring out the greatness in you.

We encourage you to attend at least one talk a month by people such as these. After hearing twelve talks from twelve different great and inspiring presenters, you will find that one or more has really gotten inside you and given you a glimpse of your real potential. Once you glimpse your potential, you will inevitably begin moving forward to fulfilling it, and you will just as inevitably discover that prosperity will begin coming your way.

Place two fingers on your chest and say out loud, "I'm pushing back my limits. I'm going to find out what my real abilities are!"

Of course, you may not always or even frequently have access to speakers. Therefore, we suggest you buy and listen to their audiocassette tapes. Become a positive tape addict. Tapes can change your life. They did ours!

```
┌─────────────────────────────┐
│                             │
│         STEP 4              │
│                             │
└─────────────────────────────┘
```

Listen to Inspirational and Instructional Tapes

Every human alive, barring the hearing-impaired, can benefit from audiotapes. When tape listening becomes a habit and a hobby, it can lift our lives when we're down and out. We know this because it happened to us.

Shortly after Mark went bankrupt, he was in the pits just about as low as it was possible to get. He was so far down, in fact, that he might have stayed there permanently if it hadn't been for tapes.

Some time earlier he had been given a tape by Cavett Robert, the dean of American speakers. At the time, he didn't listen to it because he didn't realize its value to him. Mark didn't understand that it had the power to change his life from bad to good. But when he was bankrupt, he needed all the support he could find, so he listened to the tape, "Are You the Cause or the Effect?" He played it over and over again until he could virtually recall it word-for-word by memory. Then he got other tapes. He was pulled up from the bottom by tapes. They literally saved his life.

Jack had a similar experience listening to Mark Victor Hansen's tape set "How to Outperform Yourself." He listened to it at least fifty times. The ideas on prosperity consciousness and peak performance became indelibly imprinted in his subconscious mind. In the next two years Jack tripled his income!

We truly understand what Earl Nightingale meant when he said, "Tape listening is the most important advance in technology since the invention of the printing press. The reason is that almost 100 percent of humanity's six billion people can listen—in their own language—barring only the hearing-impaired." Of course he meant that tapes could reach ten times the number that the printed word could reach.

Tapes Are Quick

It doesn't take long to listen to a tape. An investment of thirty minutes a day listening to tapes over the course of a year adds up to one full month of forty-hour work-weeks of listening. It can be done driving to and from work. As Cavett Robert says, "Make your driving time learning time. Get a classroom on wheels!" Another alternative is to tone your mind while toning your muscles—listen to great tapes while working out or running.

Repetition is the key here. Dr. Maxwell Maltz discovered that it takes twenty-one days of consecutive listening to the same message before we adopt it as our own. When Mark bought a new car not long ago, for example, he discovered that the designers had switched the skyroof button from the ceiling, where it had been in his old car, to the dashboard. For roughly twenty-one days his subconscious had him reaching for the roof.

When Jack bought a new house recently, he was halfway home on the freeway to his old house before he realized he was driving in the wrong direction. He did this for several days.

Have you ever noticed that it is about January 21 before you start putting the correct year on your checks when you are filling in the date? It takes just about that time—twenty-one days—to change a mental habit!

Ultimately, you'll want to make your own tapes to listen to! You can tell yourself whatever you want to hear, and then listen to it over and over again. One of our colleagues plays subliminal music on four self-made, positive-message tapes. His results, he tells us, are fantastic.

Use Tapes with the Family

The question most often asked at our seminars is "What do I do for my negative son, daughter, wife or husband?" The answer is, play positive tapes in your car while they are a captive audience with you. Ralph Ford, a State Farm Insurance salesman in Missouri, heard Mark for the first time several years ago, so he bought a set of his tapes and proceeded to listen as he drove his family around. They were resistant at first, but eventually they surrendered to listening. As a result, his wife upped her self-esteem and lost thirty-one pounds in six months. His eighth-grade son had pulmonary asthma and was failing academically; tapes changed his mental picture of himself.

His son approached his coach and asked, "If I get good grades, can I play a quarter of basketball, rest a quarter and then play another quarter?" He could, and did.

Ralph's daughter, Jill, was eleven years old and five feet, eleven inches tall. She was taking dance classes and wanted to dance on Broadway. Her dance instructor said, "She's too tall, gangly and uncoordinated." The tapes said, "Don't listen to negative, self-destructive input, no matter from what source."

Today she is a wonderful, elegant dancer and model.

As for Ralph himself, he's doubled his income since he started listening to tapes.

Tapes can change *your* life, too.
Here are some of the best tapes available:

Visualizing Is Realizing, by Mark Victor Hansen
Available from M. V. Hansen & Associates, Inc.
P.O. Box 7665, Newport Beach, CA 92659
Call 1-800-433-2314

Self-Esteem and Peak Performance,
by Jack Canfield (Career Track)

Available from the Canfield Group
6035 Bristol Parkway, Culver City, CA 90230
Call 1-800-2-ESTEEM

How to Build High Self-Esteem, by Jack Canfield
(Nightingale-Conant)

*Chicken Soup for the Soul: 101 Stories to Open the Heart and
Rekindle the Spirit*, by Jack Canfield and Mark Victor Hansen

---

STEP 5

Attend Seminars

We have our office staff attend at least one inspirational and
education seminar each month. Our thought is that if they're
growing on the inside, it will show up on the outside. Positive
thinkers at seminars reinforce your self-esteem and underwrite your conception of what's possible. Life experiences
have a tendency to downplay the positive, eradicate it and
level you down to the status quo. Seminars will push you back
up above the mundane.

> *The subconscious mind operates on the law of be-
> lief. You do whatever you really believe you will
> do. Believe it, and it will happen.*

The greatest opportunities for seminars are in an educational setting. What is a college class if not an extended seminar? We always suggest that college and university students think about the time they spend in their classes. It can be the most productive time of their educational careers. We also tell them to pick their classes according to who is teaching, not according to the subject. Great instructors, whether in a school or a formal seminar, can produce great results. Find and study under great and inspiring speakers and teachers.

STEP 6

Avoid the Influence of Bad TV

In the average American home, the TV set is on about 7.2 hours a day. On the average, children spend two hours more a day watching TV than they spend in a classroom. TV has become the real teacher of the minds of our children—and ourselves. As managers of ourselves and our children, we need to ask, "Is the show I am about to watch, or let my child watch, teaching and modeling behavior that I want to duplicate or participate in?"

If it isn't, do we really want to watch it? Our recommendation is that we selectively restrict the quantity and quality of our TV viewing. It's not that TV is intrinsically bad. It's just that it's abused and overused. Here are some techniques that may help:

1. *Try a TV "moratorium."* Shut it off for one whole week. Allow no TV viewing by any member of the family. A friend of ours carried seven TVs out of his home into his garage. He substituted "family time," a night when every family member is present and can invite guests. Communication, games and interaction are the rule. The

family loved it and continued a modified form of it for the next decade. They now watch TV only one night a week.

2. *Check your TV guide first.* Don't simply turn on the set to see what's on. Check out the good programs in advance and mark them. Then either make it a point to be there to see them, or record them on a VCR. The point is that planned TV makes for better TV.

3. *Rent videotapes.* Don't make it a habit to watch most network programming. Most network programs and sitcoms play to the lowest common demoninator. Instead, rent uplifting, educational programs and world-class dramas. That way you can make the most of the time you spend in front of the tube.

4. *Consider getting a satellite dish.* Even with scrambling, there's a great deal available—nearly a hundred channels as of this writing. A great deal of it is entertaining and educational. And it's usually much better than what's available on cable. The Advent Direct Satellite Broadcast means more options for everyone.

Mind Power: A Terrible Thing to Waste

Your mind is the most powerful tool in the universe. It can reach out and touch the stars or plumb the ocean's depths. It can conceptualize micro-events and macro-events. If it were a computer, we've been told, it would fill the entire state of Texas!

Perhaps the best way to see the true value of our minds is to realize what life would be like if we were unable to use them. Naomi Rhode tells the story of a man she met on a trip to China. He was a Chinese citizen working in a Friendship Store. She was buying souvenirs and was astonished to discover that he spoke excellent English. He asked where she had recently been. She said she had seen the Great Wall, and asked when the last time was he had been to see it.

"Alas," he replied, "I have not seen it and cannot see it."

He explained that he had the equivalent of a master's degree, yet he had been assigned the job of a clerk in the store. He had to work about eight hours a day and had only one day off a month. Travel was out of the question.

Naomi asked, "What is your greatest dream?"

He immediately replied, "To live in America—the land of opportunity."

"Why?" Naomi asked.

"Because in America you can do what you want, when you want, with whom you want, as much as you want."

It's so easy to expand and fill our minds here. So easy that we often take it for granted and waste that priceless opportunity. You have a brilliant and wonderful mind, the marvel of the universe. Use it and improve it.

12

Awakening Our Spiritual Selves

Often we see plaques on the walls of people's homes that read, "God first, family second, work third." That's wrong. It's wrong as a credo because they are all first. We are spiritual beings living in a spiritual universe. That spirituality permeates our families, our work and our entire lives. Our choice is to recognize it and work with it, or deny it and have it work against us.

A Spiritual World

In work, in finance, in health, in many areas of our lives, we use terms that we all immediately recognize. When we get to spirituality, there is frequently disagreement over terminology.

We're sure that many readers are already wondering, What do Mark and Jack mean by "spirituality"?

That reminds us of the lady in San Francisco who was living in a suite at the fabulous Fairmont Hotel. The cost was astronomical and she began to feel guilty about spending all that money on herself. So one day, as she was exiting the hotel, she saw a disheveled bum stumbling down the street, and the spirit moved her. She walked up to him, put a hundred-dollar bill in his hand and said, "Godspeed, my man."

The next day, as she was coming out of the hotel, a nicely dressed, cleanly shaven man walked up to her, placed five hundred-dollar bills in her hand and said, "Godspeed paid five to one!"

Which, we suppose, goes to show that one person's spirituality is another person's racehorse. Therefore, let's define spirituality before we move a step further.

To us, spirituality involves more than the mind or the intellect; it involves the soul. When we do something spiritual, we do it from our souls. But please be sure to understand that when we speak of spiritual matters, we're not speaking of religious dogma. We believe religions do address the spiritual, but the spiritual can also be addressed secularly.

Awakening Our Spirituality

Each of us has a spiritual side of our being. Finding it, however, can sometimes be a long and arduous process. Buckminster Fuller, for example, never discovered his spiritual being until his bleakest hour. One of his daughters had died. His business had failed. He was ostracized from the intellectual community and considered a foolish "Yankee Tinkerer." So he decided to end it all by drowning himself in Lake Michigan. Standing on the edge, ready to commit suicide, he asked himself, "Is there a God? Do I have a purpose in life?"

Intuitively and spontaneously, the answer came back,

"There *is* an intelligence in the universe, and your job is to dedicate yourself to humanity's comprehensive welfare on spaceship Earth."

Thoughts of suicide vanished. He was now purposeful, moving forward. He never stopped or swayed from his purpose from that day forward.

Mark's spiritual awakening was also a long time coming. It didn't come from religion when he was a child. His family attended an orthodox church in the Midwest. Everyone seemed to take a snooze during the sermon. His reaction was to think that religion put people to sleep. Mark reflects:

"When I talked with my friends, our common experience was that church told us, 'Don't do this and don't do that.' Consequently, our experiences were essentially negative and unfulfilling. The early consensus of my colleagues was that maybe they didn't need to get involved in that aspect of their lives.

"But then, shortly after I went bankrupt, two friends invited me to hear Dr. Norman Vincent Peale at his famous Marble Collegiate Church in Manhattan. It was a vibrant and uplifting experience for me. Dr. Peale wanted to 'love people into heaven.' He was feeding his congregants spiritual vitamins, infusing them with a vital life-giving enthusiasm. His sermon made me aware of a spiritual void which I then desperately wanted to fill.

"Next my two friends took me to lunch and said that for kicks we should go see Reverend Ike in Washington Heights, New York. Reverend Ike is the black 'money minister' who says, 'I'm black when it's convenient. The rest of the time, I'm green!' When we arrived for the afternoon service, I was astounded to see so many elegant, chauffeur-driven limousines bringing in the congregants. Once inside I found that the environment was a strange combination of lavish opulence and tasteful reverence.

"Five thousand people filled his United Palace to overflowing. We were three white men visiting a predominantly black church for the first time. We were loved, hugged, kissed and welcomed. No one knew or cared that I had gone bankrupt just days before. There was a feeling that everyone was growing and knowing spiritually.

"When Reverend Ike talked, he ignited my spiritual spark plug. He provided me with exciting new insights into spiritual teaching. I discovered that my bankruptcy had put my mind, soul and spirit in bondage. I wanted to be free spiritually and economically. He said, 'God is rich. He created the universe and all that's in it. God is infinite. You have God in you, so you have infinite creative possibilities within you.'

"Wow! I could feel the spirit moving within me (and it is a *felt* experience). My spiritual side was being awakened for the first time, and I was on my way toward becoming a spiritual person."

Jack's spiritual awakening occurred during a yoga class in Western Massachusetts. He reflects:

"When I was in high school, I was very much into church. Our whole family went to church. It is just what we did. But I got turned off by the inter-denominational pettiness I observed in the church elders. If God was so all-loving, how could the Presbyterians think the Catholics were so bad? God was such a grand idea, but the church was so petty. I loved how I felt singing in the youth choir, where the spirit of God flowed through us, but church had become shallow and petty to me.

"When I went off to Harvard, I read Bertrand Russell and decided I was an agnostic. I wasn't sure that God did or didn't exist. But in graduate school at the University of Massachusetts I took a yoga class to become more relaxed.

"During one of those yoga classes, our instructor was leading us through a meditation and I had a direct experience of God. I knew without any doubt that God existed and flowed through all living things. I was in a state of rapture and bliss that lasted for hours afterward. Later I had many similar expe-

riences which reinforced and reconfirmed my understanding
of God. That knowledge that we are all one in spirit and that
God is Love has guided all my actions ever since.

"I now belong to a church that is more reflective of my
needs. The congregation is extremely multi-cultural, with
whites, blacks, Hispanics and Asians, all strongly repre-
sented. Each has brought a unique gift of spirit. The black
Baptist gospel singing, the deep and penetrating meditation
periods, the love of family, the wisdom of Christ and the spirit
of love that prevails at every service is a powerful mix of all
aspects of the spiritual experience I seek."

Your Spiritual Needs

Each of us has a spiritual aspect, but that aspect and how we
address it can differ remarkably. We've indicated how it was
for three people we've known very well—Bucky Fuller and
ourselves. For you it may be totally different.

Your own spiritual awakening and purpose may also be far
different from our experiences, but like Mark's and Bucky
Fuller's, may come about because of some traumatic experience. This was most dramatically illustrated in the movie *Res-
urrection*. Ellen Burstyn plays the role of a lady who totally
adores her husband, a blue-collar worker. She works part-time
without his knowledge and saves up enough money to buy him
the red sports car of his dreams. She delivers it to him as he
leaves for work.

He is blissed-out with the gift. They immediately hop in
and take the car for a spin. As they are careening around the
California hilltop corners, a child on a skateboard suddenly
gets in their way. To avoid hitting him, they drive off the road,
plunge down a long, steep cliff into the ocean and into what
looks like certain death.

In the next scene they are trying to save the Ellen Burstyn
character's life. One doctor says, "We're losing her." They

administer electric shock. She is saved, but is told she'll never walk again.

Now an amazing spiritual transformation takes place. Burstyn's character heals herself. She suddenly can walk. Then she begins to heal others. Suddenly sick people are brought to her en masse. Her healing abilities are scientifically tested at UCLA: tested, believed, but not understood. She, however, understands that it's her own spirituality that has been awakened, that has given her the newfound gift of healing.

Very few of us have such a dramatic spiritual awakening. At some point in our lives, most of us will have some sort of high-consciousness experience, and often that will lead into the most significant phase of our life.

As we've seen, it can be brought out by some kind of trauma. It can also arise from a disability. The lives of Stevie Wonder and Ray Charles illustrate this dramatically. Each lost his external sense of sight, only to see more clearly with an "inner eye," and emerge to share profound music.

In the Special Olympics for the physically disabled, spirituality surges to the fore. Often a child who is running in first place will fall down, and his compatriots, instead of rushing by and claiming victory for themselves, will stop and give aid, picking him up and sending him victoriously forward. If you've never attended a Special Olympics, we heartily encourage you to do so. You can't help but be moved by the courage, love and generosity of spirit that abounds at such an event.

The awakening of our spiritual side, no matter what the circumstances, is always a precursor to future greatness. This is seen in great leaders such as Albert Einstein, Abraham Lincoln, Ralph Waldo Emerson, Martin Luther King, Jr., Mother Teresa and thousands of others. Each felt spiritually awakened and believed that his or her accomplishments were directed by a greater force operating spiritually in the universe. They felt they could personally tap into that force and use it. This

same force exists for you and me. It's just waiting for us to
awaken to it.

Spiritual Techniques

There are a number of steps we can all take to add a sense of
spirituality to our lives. These are simple things, yet their results will bring harmony and balance to all other aspects of
your life.

1. *Say an original, hand-holding grace over each meal.* Expressing gratitude for the food we eat uplifts the spirit—and
even makes the meal taste better! We also recommend a
practice that we learned from Bob Gore, a friend of ours
from North Carolina. Bob suggested, "Put your hands on
the opposite edges of your meal plate. Have your palms face
each other and mentally send white-light energy through
your food. Mentally and spiritually let your 'inner knower'
know that you only want to eat food that is nourishing, safe
and healthful for your body." We believe this process not
only helps to avoid indigestion and possibly even food poi-
soning, but uplifts us spiritually as well.

Take a moment also to thank God and all the people that
have contributed to your having this food: the farmer who
grew it; the people who processed it, transported it, and
prepared it for your consumption. Sometimes, when we're
feeling especially grateful, we even acknowledge the worms
who created the proper aeration for the soil so the seeds
could grow into plants. Gratitude, we believe, is one of the
highest spiritual principles.

2. *Seek to find your spiritual purpose in life.* We've talked
before about purpose in many places in this book. It's important, however, once we find our purpose in life, for us to
imbue it with spiritual overtones. If it is to be achievable—
and worth achieving—our purpose must serve humanity

and be spiritual in nature. Having only a self-serving purpose is simply self-defeating.

> *The Dead Sea is dead only because it takes in*
> *water and doesn't give any out. It's constipated*
> *and congested. One of life's great laws is the law*
> *of circulation. Keep circulating good, and good*
> *will keep circulating you.*

We believe that seeking a spiritual purpose has led to the
hospice movement, which is founded on the belief that no one
should die alone. Through a hospice, we can arrange to have
our loved ones hold our hands on the way out of this physical
life. The hospice movement acknowledges that death is a part
of life's continuum. That is essentially a spiritual belief.

In the book *Closer to the Light,* Dr. Melvin Morse writes
about children who have had near-death experiences. They
have been in a coma, or briefly pronounced clinically dead,
only to be revived. In each case they reported seeing the Light
on the other side. They had seen directly into the world of
spirit. What we found most interesting was Dr. Morse's conclusion: that a family's sharing in the death experience is an
important spiritual rite of passage for the survivors, because
when the one who is dying experiences the Light, everyone
who is present shares the experience. It strengthens their faith
that there is indeed a spiritual reality. Unfortunately, he also
reports that when the patient is drugged out on morphine or
Demerol, the patient's subtle sensory system is numbed out
and both the one who is dying and the family members are
denied this important spiritual awareness. What a shame!
That is why we are such firm supporters of the hospice movement.

3. *Develop a spiritual understanding of life and death.* It's
our belief that at death we make a transition to another
phase of life. We're absolutely certain of it, and we draw
strength from that knowledge. If we didn't have such a
belief, there would be an empty spot, a vacuum in our
spiritual lives that would be continually sucking energy
from us. Resolving that question in our minds frees us
from the fear of death to give our best energy to embrac-
ing life.

4. *Look for a minister, priest, rabbi or other teacher to facilitate your spiritual growth.* We've never met a truly great
person who didn't have a great and inspiring spiritual
mentor. Bucky Fuller said that when he met Albert Einstein, the man "glowed." "Light emanated from his
countenance. He was tuned into the universe and God
in a profound way." That's why he was a great teacher.
Be sure, when you select your spiritual teacher, that you
match your feeling nature with his or hers. Regardless
of the message, it will be lost if you communicate on
different levels of feeling.

5. *Do spiritual things.* These can be immediate and personal, or they can be magnanimously social. One immediate personal thing we can do is to give away all our
used—or unused—clothing to charity. It'll make you
feel better about your own good fortune. (And you can
deduct a portion of the cost of the donated clothes from
your income taxes!)

Doing spiritual things in a social context can also produce
amazing results both for ourselves and others. One such act is
the Make a Wish Foundation. They help make wishes come
true for children who are terminally ill.

We can do something similar, depending on our circumstances. One true and heartrending account happened to a
young mother and her seven-year-old son, Bopsy, in Phoenix,

Arizona. Bopsy was terminally ill with an incurable disease. His mother had the presence of mind to ask him, "If you could make one wish and know that it would come true, what would you want?"

"I'd want to be a fireman," he replied.

With a deep desire to fulfill her son's wish, she appealed to the local fire chief, who had a big, loving, compassionate heart. He said, "You have Bopsy ready tomorrow morning at 7 A.M. and we will pick him up with the hook-and-ladder truck and he'll be honorary fire chief for a day. If you'll give me his measurements, we'll make him a hard hat like we wear and a yellow fire coat and galoshes too!"

Bopsy was taken out a few days later on three real fire calls. As a result he was inspired to live three months longer than any doctor had predicted he would. On the day he died, the head nurse on Bopsy's floor read on the monitor that his vital signs were weakening. She called the fire chief and told him that she didn't think the boy would be much longer in this world. She said that she thought it would be better for him if he passed on with people he loved around him. "Chief, is there anything you can do to make his transition out of life less painful and more joyous?"

The fire chief said, "You bet there is. Tell him to hold on. We'll be there in less than five minutes. Tell the other patients that they'll hear the sirens and see the lights flashing, but not to be concerned. The hospital isn't on fire. We're just coming to see Bopsy one last time. Oh, and open his third-story window because we're coming in on the hook-and-ladder!"

Fourteen firefighters, men and women, climbed the ladder and entered Bopsy's room. Each of them hugged him, cajoled him, caressed and cuddled him with tears in all their eyes. He finally looked up and said, "Am I really a fireman now?"

Pushing back tears, the chief said, "Yes, Bopsy."

And then he died.

We conclude with this dramatic story because each of us

has a little child within us with a spiritual wish that remains to be fulfilled. We would ask that you spend the rest of your life fulfilling the wish of that little boy or little girl inside of you.

Conclusion

Our goal in writing this book was simply to turn you on to more and more and better and better. To show you that life's abundance is available to you just for the asking. If there's a single insight that we would love to have you come away with, it's that *You can change your life by changing the way you think about life.*

Put into your conscious mind whatever it is that you want to achieve, and your subconscious will do the rest for you. Use the three keys of writing down your goals, then visualizing and affirming them, to unlock the conscious mind and get it going in the right direction. Give it the "what" and watch your "inner knower" supply the "how" to achieve the greatness that's inside you.

We want to leave you with the inspiring story of little Markita Andrews, a true superstar. Markita is a girl who lived in difficult circumstances. Her father had left home, and her mother was working hard as a waitress to support both of them.

Her mother told Markita that she was saving her money so that the little girl could go to college. Because her mother had always dreamed of traveling and kept travel pictures around their home, she was also saving the money to take them on a trip around the world.

Now, most children would have listened and not heard. But Markita heard and decided that she could and would do something to make these dreams a reality. But, of course, she was only a little girl. What could she do?

As a Girl Scout, Markita read that if she sold enough Girl Scout cookies, she'd win a trip to camp. But if she sold more than anyone else ever had, she'd win a trip around the world for herself and her mom.

Did she want to sell Girl Scout cookies? Not really.

Did she want that trip? You betcha!

She wrote down that she would sell more Girl Scout cookies than anyone else. She visualized and dreamed it. She affirmed in front of her aunt that she would do it, and her aunt gave her some good advice: "Go where the people with money are and ask them to buy cookies."

Markita stood in the lobby of a different apartment building in New York City, between 4:30 and 6:30 in the late afternoon. She approached prospective buyers politely, warmly and with a smile, saying, "I'm earning a trip to camp. Would you like to invest in one dozen Girl Scout cookies or two dozen?"

After *five years* of selling, she had sold 42,000 boxes of Girl Scout cookies! She took her mother on that trip around the world. Her fame spread. IBM asked her to talk to their salespeople. She also talked to the insurance business' "Million Dollar Round Table," and while she was there, she sold to the five thousand top life insurance agents in attendance one box of cookies each!

So amazing were her results that Walt Disney Productions made a movie about her called *The Cookie Kid.* Her book, *How to Sell More Cookies, Condos, Cadillacs, Computers . . . And Everything Else,* became a nationwide best-seller.

Amazing results! All by a little girl selling cookies.

You can have amazing results, too! We know you can. Now *you* know you can. So what are you waiting for?

Dare to *win!*